HCB-ANGUS
FIRE ENGINE BUILDERS

LET OUR EXPERIENCE
BE YOUR GUARANTEE

H.C.B. ENGINEERING LTD.
TOTTON · SOUTHAMPTON
TELEPHONE: TOTTON 3141

HCB-ANGUS
FIRE ENGINE BUILDERS

AIDAN FISHER

AMBERLEY

This book is dedicated to all those fire fighters, men and women, from over 100 countries who were the company's market who have ridden on, and worked with, fire engines built by HCB-Angus and to those craftspeople from in and around Totton who built them and the commercial vehicles that largely preceded them.

Front Cover
Scammel Nubian Mk 2 crash tender registered 960 DZB, s5929, served its entire career with Air Rianta at Cork Airport. The appliance was the prototype to this specification and was purchased by Air Rianta before completion.

Rear Cover
One of the many HCB-Angus Bedford TK water tender sets off on a shout on a mucky night. A scene oft repeated over the years by these dependable fire engines in many countries of the world and, indeed, still being repeated even now.

First published 2012

Amberley Publishing
The Hill, Stroud
Gloucestershire, GL5 4EP

www.amberley-books.com

Copyright © Aidan Fisher 2012

The right of Aidan Fisher to be identified as the Author
of this work has been asserted in accordance with the
Copyrights, Designs and Patents Act 1988.

All rights reserved. No part of this book may be reprinted
or reproduced or utilised in any form or by any electronic,
mechanical or other means, now known or hereafter invented,
including photocopying and recording, or in any information
storage or retrieval system, without the permission in writing
from the Publishers.

British Library Cataloguing in Publication Data.
A catalogue record for this book is available from the British Library.

ISBN 978 1 4456 0535 7

Typeset in 10pt on 12pt Sabon.
Typesetting and Origination by Amberley Publishing.
Printed in the UK.

Contents

	Introduction and Acknowledgements	7
1.	The Company History	9
2.	Vehicle Production	21
3.	Commercial Vehicle Bodybuilding	24
4.	The Early Days and into the 1950s	30
5.	The 1960s	43
6.	The 1970s	62
7.	The 1980s	89
8.	The 1990s – the Final Years	117
	Postscript	128

FIREFLY
ERF TYPE 'B' APPLIANCE

A new conception in major appliances employing the latest design features developed by HCB-ANGUS LTD. and ERF LTD. to meet requirements of fire brigades in the larger towns and cities.

- Perkins V8 diesel engine developing 170 B.H.P.

- Double stepped chassis frame giving low entry and efficient handling under full loading capacity.

HCB-ANGUS LTD

Introduction and Acknowledgements

This story comes about almost by accident. It was in the mid-1970s, when I was part of the preservation fraternity restoring and exhibiting stationary engines, that a chance conversation with a fellow exhibitor revealed that where he was working an old fire engine was to be thrown away for no better reason than that they had broken the pump. Enquiries were made and I found myself owning Bedford S CDM 289, ex Birkenhead Fire Brigade and Kodak (Kirkby) Ltd. Contact was made with HCB-Angus, the builders, all was refurbished, and the engine was rallied for some years.

Changes in circumstance necessitated that the engine should go and there the matter rested. Eventually withdrawal symptoms set in and Bedford TJ CBF 689, ex Staffordshire Fire Brigade, also by HCB-Angus, became mine. Later again this fire engine was replaced with Bedford TK SAG 982J, ex the southwestern area of Scotland, and lastly by the almost unique Morris FGK 40 BAA 778C, ex J. S. Fry (Chocolate Makers) Bristol, both of which were also by HCB-Angus.

Enquiries of the company revealed that all their records were with the late Alan Gartside – and eventually with me! Some 900 paper files and twenty-two rolls of microfilm were patiently read through and catalogued, blank spaces filled in over many years and a database created.

When the company closed down they were good enough to give me everything they had, photographs, technical papers, brochures and bits and pieces, and it is this material that forms the basis of this work.

I have to thank Richard Anning, buying manager for the company from 1964 until they closed, for being my contact point with the company and for patiently answering my endless questions over the years; Niel Steele, Andy Anderson, Roger Mardon, Ted Angus, Ian Moore and many others for filling in and making sense of the gaps in the database; and the many enthusiasts from all over the country and the rest of the world who have provided snippets of information and photographic evidence to further clarify the picture.

The photographs used in this volume have come from the library maintained by the company in the vast majority of instances. Where photographs from others have been used they are acknowledged with thanks and in the odd instance where the origin is unknown, this is stated.

Appliances are referred to throughout the text by their body serial number, e.g. s3456, and this will enable the reader to cross reference with the database.

Thanks go to my publisher Campbell McCutcheon and Amberley Publishing for their help and guidance in the book's production.

Aidan Fisher
Manchester
January 2012

1
The Company History

The 1930s were difficult times. The Great Depression was barely over and work was hard to come by, yet the motor trade was in full swing. The concept of unitary construction, where there is no separate chassis but all the body and frame are all one, was well under way but there were plenty of cars and vans still being produced in chassis and body form.

Against this background a Mr A. Niblett set up business in Grosvenor Square, Southampton repairing accident-damaged bodywork and creating new bodies, particularly on light vans and trucks. Mr Niblett had served his time with the Humber car company and was a skilled coachbuilder of the old school. When he required sheet metal or engineering work, he sub-contracted this out to a local company, L. E. Young Ltd.

It is reputed, though no pictorial evidence survives to corroborate this, that they produced as a collaborative effort a forward control conversion of the 1930s Trojan van, and later on the Ford A series commercial vehicles. It was against this background of inventive body building that Mr Nibblet's company, calling itself Hampshire Car Bodies and Renovators, made its first foray into the fire appliance world. Criterion Garage, Southampton received an order for an appliance from Southampton Fire Brigade in 1933, followed shortly after by one for Southampton Aerodrome. These will be looked at later in more detail. In 1939, just before the Second World War, the companies joined forces while retaining their identities, and left central Southampton and moved out to Totton, which became the home of the company for the rest of its production life.

With the onset of war, in common with all manufacturing industry, domestic production ceased and all efforts were devoted to war production. Hampshire Car Bodies and Renovators became involved in the building of the tail section of Horsa gliders as well as doing some commercial vehicle body repair work for the Ministry of Transport and L. E. Young used their metalworking skills in the production of such mundane, but essential, artefacts as ammunition boxes and the like.

In the aftermath of the Second World War things were very difficult in many respects, particularly with materials and the run-down state of industry in the post-war era. All

The Horsa glider was used by the Allies for moving troops into attack during the Second World War. The company built an unknown number of tail sections, designed to detach from the main fuselage. (*Unknown photographer*)

sorts of manufactory were tried: doors, etc. for the building trade; school furniture; pattern making; and some experimental work such as beer barrels with laminated staves rather than solid wood. At a personal level, Mr Niblett died in 1946 and his shares were subsequently purchased by Adam (New Forest) Ltd. At much the same time Mr Young left his company to try his hand in Australia and Adam (New Forest) Ltd acquired L.E.Young also. Materials were in short supply and vehicle chassis were almost impossible to source (unless war surplus) as most manufacturers could not get enough for themselves, never mind supplying to third-party body builders, so other avenues had to be tried. Under the leadership of Adam (New Forest), Hampshire Car Bodies and Renovators had a go at building model boats of a very high quality, including a clinker-built model yacht whose sails were made by an unidentified famous Isle of Wight sailmaker and an engine-powered model torpedo boat, but this was not a success and the venture folded. A return was made to what they did best – building motor vehicle bodies – and a contract was successfully obtained in 1947 for the production of a thousand cabs for AEC's Monarch and Matador and then a further thousand for the Thornycroft Nippy.

As a speculative venture, in 1949 the company had a go at building a fire appliance based on the Commer QX chassis cab, which had been announced in February of 1948. This was built as a Type A water tender and was sold before completion to Berkshire and Reading Fire Brigade. On the basis of this success a second appliance was built, in this case a pump escape appliance, which was also sold before completion, to the same brigade. This experience, limited as it was, convinced the board that this was a

A picture from the September 1947 edition of the AEC in-house magazine detailing, and commenting on, the production by HCB Engineering of a cab per day as a sub-contract from AEC. (*AEC house magazine*)

field in which the company and its skills could do well. Successes took the company onto the road to its future – building fire appliances. To this end, Adam (New Forest) Ltd, owners of Hampshire Car Bodies and L. E. Young, re-organised the pair as HCB Engineering Ltd (subsequently referred to as HCB), with a commitment to the fire appliance market. However, the commercial vehicle body manufacturing arm of the company continued to thrive and produce vehicles until 1964. This in part was due to local authority financial rules whereby material ordered in a financial year had to be delivered and paid for by the end of that financial year – the end of March. This would see fire engine building at panic levels during February and March and then a fallow period until new orders started filtering through in the next financial year. This was not the case with commercial bodies for private customers, which balanced out the work rate.

In the early 1950s the company brought Bayley Ladders within their fold, thus ensuring a steady supply of 30 and 35-foot wooden trussed ladders. This arrangement did not last more than a decade and the ladder division was bought by one of the ladder makers from the company and continued independently for many years as trussed ladder suppliers to all fire appliance builders.

The 1950s were busy times indeed, with the majority of fire brigades anxious to replace their pre-war and wartime appliances, all of which were well worn. The company was, however, dividing its time, building commercial vehicle bodies and fire appliances side by side. Apart from one foray into the market abroad with a small order for Singapore, by way of the UK Crown Agency, the UK market was the centre of the company's activities. For reasons that are not apparent, records of fire appliance construction were meticulously kept after the first few months of production, but records of commercial production were not – or they were destroyed, possibly at the

The cast metal plaque fitted to the cab head rail of commercial vehicles and later to fire appliances. The blank section was stamped up with the vehicle's body serial number once this system was up and running. (*Author*)

time that production ceased. During the years up to 1960 approximately one fire appliance per week was built, together with an unknown number of commercials.

The year 1964 saw a change in fortune; George Angus & Co. Ltd, Newcastle upon Tyne, which already owned Fire Armour Ltd, formed in 1952, bought a 30 per cent stake in HCB. Fire Armour was based in Willesden in London and had produced few vehicles for the home market but had extensive contacts abroad, where they made the majority of their sales. This joining up had a number of repercussions:
1) The name HCB-Angus Ltd was adopted, though the trademark 'Firefly' that had been used by Fire Armour now appeared on HCB-Angus appliances and continued to do so until 1968.
2) Fire Armour ceased to trade as fire appliance builders
3) Fire Armour's overseas expertise and order books were incorporated into activities at Totton to give HCB-Angus Ltd a wider operating base.
4) Commercial vehicle bodybuilding ceased.

This enabled the new company to rationalise its activities and really spread its wings in the fire appliance world with production of fire appliances stepped up to meet the needs of the expanded market. The construction of commercial vehicle bodies ceased immediately (it is understood that the last item produced by this arm of the company was, in fact, a chicken plucking machine!)

The 1960s were busy times for HCB-Angus, with production of appliances ramping up threefold and activities spreading around the world until some 111 countries had

The cast radiator grill badge as fitted after the collaboration with Angus Fire in 1964. (*Author*)

This style of radiator badge became the style post-1967 but appeared in several colour ways and sizes over the years. (*Author*)

The vehicle plate adopted after the 1964 merger. By and large, this plate was found on the nearside rear and on the inside of the officers' cab door. This plate, 6267.2, is from one of the Dorset Fire and Rescue Service Bedford TK appliances, the group registered A937–A940 KJT. (*Author*)

received an HCB-Angus appliance – some had only one, such as Colombo, a dual purpose appliance built on a Bedford TK chassis, s1047, in 1965; some had hundreds, such as Nigeria, which had nearly 400 over the years in assorted specifications. All this was achieved in the factory space occupied early in the company's life, causing production to be cramped and difficult. Many appliances were completed in the yard or under makeshift covers of scaffolding and tarpaulin!

The 1960s saw an important tie up with Simon Engineering, Dudley Ltd, which was getting into its stride building hydraulic platforms, but not building bodies or undertaking fire engineering. The link-up saw Simon Engineering mounting booms on chassis and then the vehicle being brought to Totton, where HCB-Angus completed the engineering and bodywork to the customer's requirements.

Two views of the interior of the original premises at Commercial Road, Totton. Note the lack of height and the cramped working conditions. (*HCB-Angus Archive*)

The new factory at Millbrook. This base undertook all the fire engineering for all chassis and the bodybuilding for all metal constructions, the old factory continuing on with composite construction. The Bedford-chassied Simon Snorkel was destined for South Africa. (*HCB-Angus Archive*)

As the workload increased, the company expanded onto a new site without moving off the existing one. Some way up the road a new factory was constructed at Millbrook and it was on this new site that all the engineering and metal fabrication took place – the existing factory premises concentrated on traditional composite construction, utilising a timber frame and metal panelling.

It is interesting to note that the managing director of the company stated at this time that 'in a few years there will be no composite construction and we will be working totally in metal'. How wrong he was: composite construction was in use right up to the final days of the company!

There was more company manoeuvering in 1968, with Dunlop Holdings (Ltd) buying Angus Fire Armour and in so doing obtaining a 100 per cent holding in HCB-Angus, which, of course, then became a wholly owned subsidiary. It was in this year that HCB-Angus won the coveted Queen's Award for Industry for Export, no mean feat, and at that time was the only company to receive such an award for the export of fire fighting equipment. At this time some 50–60 per cent of production was being shipped overseas.

The early 1970s were difficult times. Industrial unrest in the UK led to a three-day week and rapidly rising inflation made for difficult trading conditions, yet the company pressed on and the mid-1970s found HCB-Angus in a commanding position. Production figures made 1975 the best year, with 365 appliances going out through the gates, one a day, a figure that was never again matched. The company even had its own hourly bus service to transport personnel from site to site! Many hours were lost with travelling and moving vehicles about and the decision was made to build a totally

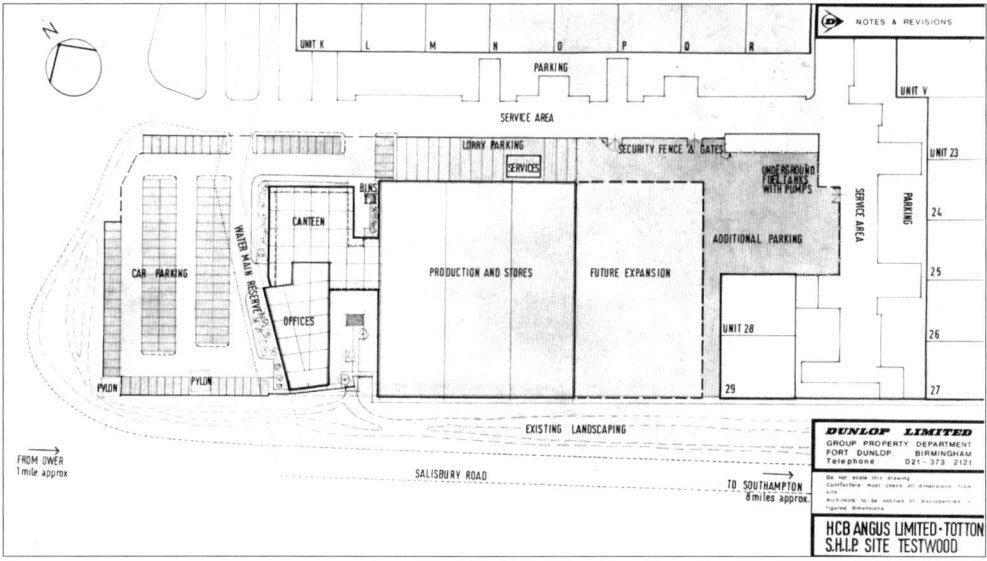

Here we have the architect's proposed plan for the new factory at the New Hampshire Industrial Park. This would give the company ample space to bring all its manufacturing to one site – with room for expansion. (*HCB-Angus Archive*)

Just one of the work areas, light and airy with ample room. Note the Morris travelling crane, a boon for weight carrying. (*HCB-Angus Archive*)

The office block just after completion with the workshops behind. The in-house magazine made great store of the fact that the company had invested in 'a computer' at the time! (*HCB-Angus Archive*)

NOTICE

HCB-Angus Limited

It is with regret that we have to announce the closure of HCB-Angus upon completion of the current outstanding orders. The closure process will be complete by the end of April 1994.

Market conditions in 1993 have given rise to substantial operating losses. This, coupled with poor prospects for 1994, have led to this regrettable decision.

We are currently in discussions with HCB-Angus employees and their union representatives in order to achieve an orderly rundown of the operation.

R.J. Rider
Director and Company Secretary
30th November 1993

Notice Boards
AFAL Directors
Heads of Department

Final confirmation of the rumours – a fax from the head office of the parent company. (*HCB-Angus Archive*)

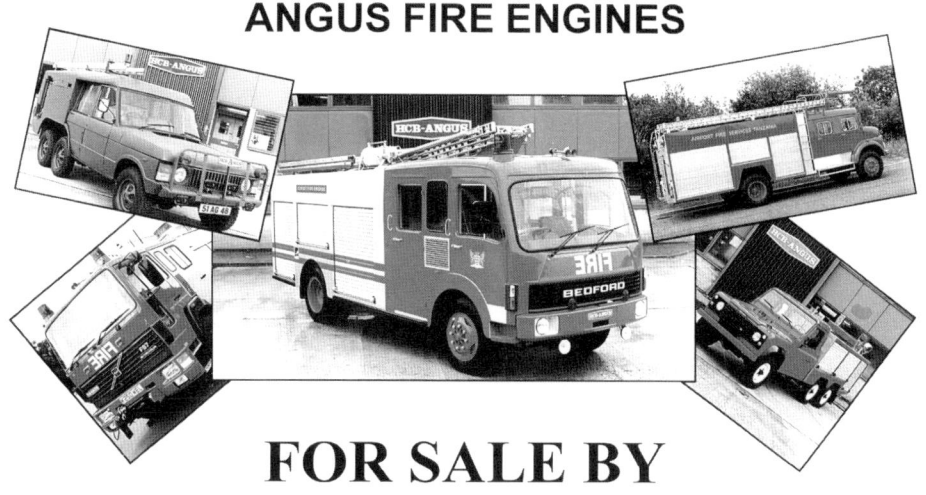

By order of the Directors, HCB Angus Ltd
following closure of their manufacturing facility of the famous

ANGUS FIRE ENGINES

FOR SALE BY AUCTION

METAL FABRICATION, ENGINEERING & WOODWORKING MACHINERY

ON: WEDNESDAY 20 JULY 1994 Commencing at 11.00 am
AT: South Hampshire Industrial Park, SOUTHAMPTON
ON VIEW: TUESDAY 19 JULY from 10.00am - 5.00pm & morning of sale from 9.00am
FINAL CLEARANCE BY 5.00 pm TUESDAY 26 JULY 1994

Catalogue Price
£2.00

EDWARD SYMMONS
& PARTNERS

Park House, Franconia Drive, Nursling, Southampton, SO16 0YW
Tel: 0703-741212   Fax: 0703-741454

The cover from the auction house catalogue listing the assets to be disposed of on 20 July 1993.
(*Reproduced with permission of E. Symonds & Partners*)

new production facility on the New Hampshire Industrial Park, Testwood, not far from the existing factories and still within Totton. Construction of the new, purpose-built offices and 100,000-square-foot works facility began in 1977 and production moved across in late 1978 with the transfer of engineering and metal fabrication from the Millbrook factory. It was not until 1981 that the woodworking facility was finally moved to Testwood and the company became wholly on one site.

Further company moves saw Guthrie Ltd, a Far Eastern engineering conglomerate company, acquire George Angus & Co. Ltd, including HCB-Angus, from Dunlop in 1980, at the start of a decade that saw difficulties for the company. There was a financial problem when the company was caught in a disastrous contract in the Far East and lost a seven-figure sum – a huge dent in their finances. Added to this, there were workforce problems and a downturn in production that brought the company to near closure but steps were taken to save the situation. As part of this rationalisation there was a reduction in size of the site operations at Totton, the office block was disposed of and the number of units on the industrial park used was reduced. This, together with a concentration on the production of local authority appliances (though not exclusively), enabled the company to continue.

In 1988 yet another change of ownership took place. This time, the British Belting Association (BBA) acquired Guthrie but HCB-Angus continued producing appliances. However, the writing was on the wall as costs continued to rise and sales continued to fall. An examination of costings by the company suggested that the 'on costs' of producing fire appliances in an area of expensive works accommodation around Southampton put approximately £1,000 onto the price of the appliance compared with the company's main competitors, a situation that could not be sustained.

Rumours persisted until it was finally confirmed, at the end of November 1993, that the company would cease trading on the completion of its order book. As it happened, the three appliances that were on order but had not been started at this time were sub-contracted out to one of company's main competitors, Saxon Ltd, and thus did not enter production.

As trades completed their final tasks they were slowly laid off until just a few key workers remained to oversee the closure and disposal of the site and its equipment. The final act took place on 24 June 1994, when all the equipment was auctioned off and the company doors closed for the last time

And so sixty plus years of production came to a close. An unknown number of commercial bodies and cab structures, together with some 6,500 fire appliances of all shapes and sizes delivered to fire brigades around the world, were surely a testament to the skills and craftsmanship of the company's craft workers and office staff.

2
Vehicle Production

As was mentioned in the company story, Hampshire Car Bodies and Renovators were typical of coachbuilders of the day, manufacturing bodies for light vans and trucks and also creating 'shooting brakes' and other specialist vehicles. As stated earlier, just two appliances were built prior to the Second World War. Southampton Appliance No. 14 was a Surrey-built Dodge and Hampshire Car Bodies and Renovators were contracted to build the body. Registered OW 4021, the appliance was fitted with a first aid pump only, with the crew space entered from the rear and facing inwards – somewhat safer than the usual Braidwood style of the day, with the crew sitting outside.

The second appliance was for the then fledgling Southampton Aerodrome after an Air Ministry inspector had reported that 'in the event of a flying accident it would be useless to rely on the Town Fire Brigade who would take fifteen minutes to reach the aerodrome'.

This second appliance was registered OW 2987, a Surrey-built Dodge similar to the Southampton City appliance, but with a 30-gallon foam extinguisher fitted - more suited to the purpose!

With the onset of war, in common with all manufacturing industry, domestic production ceased and all efforts were focussed on war production. Some work was undertaken for the repair and modification of fire appliances for the newly formed National Fire Service; just what is not clear but it is presumed that it will have been in the commonising of components and in the repair of accident-damaged appliances.

Post-war, the company speculatively built a Type A water tender on a Commer QX forward control 5–7 ton chassis which was quickly sold to Berkshire and Reading Fire Brigade. This was followed by an escape carrier that sold equally quickly, and to the same brigade. These were FBL 409 and GJB 809 respectively and were the first of many, many fire appliances to flow from the works during the next half century.

OW 4021, a Surry Dodge, purchased from Hampshire Car Bodies and Renovators, is believed to be the first domestic fire appliance built by the company. It was delivered to Southampton Fire Brigade in 1934. (*Alan House*)

OW 2987, a very similar appliance but this time modified slightly to become an airport appliance for Southampton Airport. (*Alan House*)

Right: An AEC Mandator fitted with an HCB-Angus-fabricated cab standing outside the AEC works at Southall. (*HCB-Angus Archive*)

Below: Restored during the last few years, here is MLE 441, an AEC Mammoth Major cabbed by HCB Engineering, arriving at Brighton at the end of the London to Brighton Commercial Vehicle Run. (*Photo with permission of David Christie*)

3
Commercial Vehicle Bodybuilding

At this point, it might be worth taking just a few moments to look the commercial vehicle body building side of HCB's activities. Commercial bodybuilding had always been on the basis of timber framing with a sheet metal skin, either steel or aluminium, built onto a commercially available chassis. This method was time-consuming and not particularly light in weight, particularly when using timber. The fabrication of curves involved considerable work, both on the part of the woodworker producing the frame and the sheet metalworker forming the body to fit over it. Two post-war developments changed this. These were the advent of glass-reinforced plastic (GRP) as a bodybuilding medium and metal framing, by way of extruded/pressed sections, instead of timber framing.

HCB explored both these avenues and developed a range of light vans using aluminium frame sections and body cover sections in fibreglass. Most of HCB production on this side was for local authority high-standard vehicles such as library vans or canteen vans, as well as a large number of parcels vans for the Great Western Railway. There were some oddities, such as the Muskeg for the Trans-Arctic Expedition (1958). This vehicle, while already designed to work in cold weather and snow, was made more suitable for the Arctic weather by the fitting of a heater, some additional bodywork and thermal insulation. The very last non-fire appliance item built in the works was a machine for plucking chickens in 1964. No one is quite sure how this came about.

The company approached the construction of light van-style vehicles by adopting what they called 'Thruway': the use of an easy-access sliding door for the cab, either sliding within the bodywork or to the outside of it. The principle was adopted for several makes of light to medium van.

A more radical development was the construction of fully forward control bodies on what were normal control chassis when delivered from the manufacturer. HCB worked with Vauxhall Motors in the development of the Bedford A, C, D and later TJ types to this end. The conversion was fully manufacturer supported and involved total removal of the bodywork, remounting the steering gear (with the track rod drag link reversed) to the front of the chassis, repositioning the pedals and the electrical and

Several of these Bombardier Muskeg tracked tractors came into the company to be 'arcticised' prior to use by the Commonwealth Antarctic Expedition in 1958. (*HCB-Angus Archive*)

A Morris LD van fitted with the company's 'Thruway' body, the sliding door giving easy access for deliveries. The up and own rear doors were quite a common feature in the 1950s. (*HCB-Angus Archive*)

A long wheelbase Bedford C or D series with a full forward control conversion fitted out internally as a mobile library. The company did quantities of this type of high-quality interior fitting. (*HCB-Angus Archive*)

A Bedford CA Mk 1, split screen, converted to a gown van. (*HCB-Angus Archive*)

A sales leaflet for the FG with the 'Thruway' van conversion. Interestingly, this concern for the driver's ease of working was not so considered by other vehicle builders at this time. (*HCB-Angus Archive*)

A conventional conversion with a box van rear body, this Austin FG with its 'angle plan' doors does not necessarily need the benefit of the company's sliding doors. (*HCB-Angus Archive*)

The company considered two variants for the front panel of the forward control conversion. The use of the Bedford grill is seen here. This was not adopted when this front panel was used in fire appliances, as a greater airflow was deemed necessary, so a bigger mesh grill was utilised. (*HCB-Angus Archive*)

A Morris FG with a fully coach-built body for Southampton's school meals service. Note the rather strange fibreglass moulding forming the scuttle to body shaping. (*HCB-Angus Archive*)

mechanical tweaks needed for such work. This gave an interesting driving position, with the driver sitting alongside the number two cylinder (of a big six) with the gear lever some feet behind him and, in the case of fire appliances, even further away due to the PTO gearbox. Even with the gear lever re-bent to point forward, the driver tended to need a double-jointed shoulder to effect gear changes!

As can be seen from the photographs of the commercial vehicles, the company tried two basic front-end treatments for the Bedford, one with a single curve to the front and the other with a shorter double curve. The latter was not as favoured and certainly in fire appliance construction, the single curve was the one adopted. The Bedford grille appears to have been used with commercials but this was not the case when this scuttle was used on the fire appliances; I suspect it was thought to not be sufficiently big to allow enough air through for pumping when standing with the engine working hard. These early commercials also saw the first use of GRP in body construction; the complex compound curves of the scuttle top on the Austin/Morris FG clearly demonstrate this. Just why these rather strange bumps were built in is unknown.

It was stated earlier that HCB produced a large number of cabs for AEC and Thornycroft, but these were traditional timber-framed/sheet metal-covered ones dating to the late 1940s in origin, although there is some interesting evidence of involvement with AEC in Mercury and Monarch cabs of composite construction. The photographs clearly show Mercury chassis in the HCB yard sporting a number of differing treatments of grille, trim and glazing, all based on the same base cab. Just a few photographs exist showing this grille treatment, with three vertical bars rather than one, on a working vehicle, the Phorepres Brick vehicle from the late 1950s being one. One wonders how many more there were?

The manufacture of van based vehicles continued right up until the amalgamation with Fire Armour, vans being bodied in batches of 100, the last of which was completed in 1965. It is rumoured that the profit margin on each van was just ten pounds!

HCB Engineering appears to have been involved in the design and construction of these cabs for AEC. The same basic structure is apparent, with detail changes. Only those cabs built by HCB Engineering have three slats to the radiator grill, whereas AEC only fitted one. The Phorepres vehicle is an eight-wheeler and was working at the time of the photograph. (*HCB-Angus Archive*)

4
The Early Days and into the 1950s

Before looking at fire appliance production, it is worth looking at how the company recorded its vehicle production as it is these body serial numbers that will be referred to throughout the text. Although no discrete numbering was used in the early post-war days of production, it is thought that some eighty appliances were built during this period.

1951 to 1968

As an order came in, it was given a file number and within this file each vehicle was given an individual number, and these were sequential. It is not clear at what file number this system started but the number 70 seems about correct. For example:

File 1007 (Nigeria): Body serials 2098, 2099
File 1008 (Warwickshire): Body serials 2100, 2101, 2102, 2103
File 1009 (North Yorkshire): Body serials 2104, 2105

The last in this sequence was

File 1211 (Manchester): Body serial 2542

1968 to the end of production

In 1968, at the time of the total integration of HCB-Angus within Angus Fire, the system was unified so that the file number and the vehicle numbers were the same. A sequential number identified a multi-vehicle order after the file number. The first file number under this system was 5001. For example:

File 5492 (North Yorkshire): Body serials 5492.1–3 (3 appliances)
File 5493 (Bahrain): Body serial 5493 (1 appliance)
File 5494 (Essex): Body serials 5493.1–8 (8 appliances)

The last in this series was:

File 6542 (Nigeria): Body number 6542

Notwithstanding the two appliances built pre-war (and there is no evidence to suggest that there were any others), there were in the region of eighty produced before the company became truly organised in this field.

The majority of appliances built in the late 1940s through to early 1950/51 were on Commer, Dodge and Leyland Comet chassis. The Commer was very popular; it was of forward control configuration with a slant engine which did not make too much of an intrusion into the cab and was of a suitable weight, five to seven tons, adequate for the loads imposed at that time. No other chassis manufacturer had such a competitive vehicle.

Most were water tender Type A, i.e. with only a hose reel pump, engine-driven via the gearbox, and with a light portable pump plumbed into the chassis-mounted water tank.

GXM 640, a Dodge Kew, is photographed in the yard at HCB Engineering. It came to HCB from the Isle of Wight Fire Brigade with three of its brothers to be converted from WrT A specification to WrT B specification. (*HCB-Angus Archive*)

Many local authority brigades were just beginning to re-equip themselves after the return of control from the National Fire Service in 1948 as their appliances were pre-war or wartime builds and were at the end of their useful lives. It must be remembered, however, that the financial and logistical situation being what it was, many appliances soldiered on into the 1960s.

HCB quickly established a basic design that was independent of the chassis manufacture, this by taking a chassis cowl and building a carefully swept body of pleasing lines. In the early 1950s, all appliances were fitted with traditional top-hinged lockers. An exception was Kent Fire Brigade who, with an order very early in the 1950s, specified roller shutters for the short lockers while retaining conventional slam doors for the others. Fife Fire Brigade shortly followed suit and by the end of the decade roller shutters were the norm for the majority of brigades. Having said that, Fife was to return to top-hinged lockers and was the last to specify an HCB vehicle so equipped. This was with the pair of Dodge G1313 appliances s6239.1 and 2, registered VFS 111Y and 112Y.

HCB devised a pressed aluminium shutter which, rather than rolling up in the head of the locker, was taken by guides over the top and down the back, thus releasing more space and producing a cost saving. This was produced in-house and persisted for many years, right through to the 1970s, by which time, however, the majority of appliances were being fitted with proprietary roller shutter from specialist manufacturers.

The publication of the Joint Committee on Design and Development (JCDD) specification for water tenders Type B required the main pump to be engine-driven and supplied from a vehicle-mounted tank or from an external source, which necessitated a power take off to be sourced. At first this was done by chassis mounting a transfer box (usually by Prestage) in the drive train to the back axle but HCB was soon to devise its own sandwich PTO. With this the main gearbox was moved backward to accommodate the PTO gearbox, which was arranged to simply plug into the clutch centre plate and have the gearbox input shaft similarly plug into the rear of the PTO box, the existing bolts linking the gearbox to the engine being replaced with long studs. The PTO gearbox could easily be arranged to have a ratio change to the pump drive line if the engine/pump r.p.m ratios required it. HCB did not manufacture its own PTO gearboxes; they were contracted out to the likes of David Brown, Jason Engineering, Drum Engineering and others. It is testament to these boxes that they rarely gave trouble and many are still operational today, many years later. Many other fire appliance manufacturers bought in the HCB power take off for use in their appliances - a recommendation!

The Commer came as a chassis cowl, so creating a short front end with a crew cab was easily accomplished, but those appliances built on the Comet required the normal control set up to be retained, as it was not practical to develop a forward control configuration, with the inevitable and undesirable increase in overall length.

Bedford was to provide the key to HCB's requirements with the announcement, in October 1951, of the Bedford S, the Big Bedford, The Bedford S was a step up in the medium truck market – an all-new design, it featured a strong chassis that could be had in various wheelbase lengths and fitted with a forward control cab and as a chassis/

FLB 409 is reputed to be the first appliance built speculatively on a Commer QX by HCB Engineering and was sold before completion to the Berkshire and Reading Fire Brigade. It was built to the JCDD specification as a B type water tender. (*HCB-Angus Archive*)

GJB 809 was built in much the same manner, again on a Commer QX chassis, and again sold before completion to Berkshire and Reading. This time, the appliance was built as a pump escape. (*HCB-Angus Archive*)

OKM 470 is one of many Commer 21a based appliances. Built for Kent Fire Brigade as one of their initial orders for five similar appliances, it was finished in full paint, something that was soon to start to disappear, to be replaced by plain stucco-finish aluminium. (*HCB-Angus Archive*)

scuttle version, it was perfect for fire appliance building. Powered by the Bedford five-litre overhead valve petrol engine, it was deemed to be adequately powered for the day.

HCB cut and shut chassis for many years, as it was easier and quicker to buy a long wheelbase stock chassis which automatically come with stronger suspension, dampers, etc. than it was to buy a short wheelbase to special order. One of the local scrap men did a good trade in discarded pieces of chassis frame! This redoubtable Bedford S chassis gave HCB the basis it needed to produce many hundreds of appliances in many guises.

When Bedford announced the 'A' series in 1953, HCB utilised a semi-forward control conversion on this chassis. This moved the windscreen forward over the bonnet/wing area and left a short bonnet. This conversion was in fact contracted out to Neville, a Southampton coachbuilder, and HCB built the rear end to the body. Less than a dozen of these were built as the company was working on a full forward control cab/body (as described in the last chapter) that could be mounted not only on the Bedford A and later derivatives but on the Dodge chassis.

It was decided to produce two versions of this conversion, one traditional and derived from the commercial bodybuilding cab utilising wood framing with aluminium panelling, and one wholly new, with the cab front constructed from fibreglass-reinforced plastics and an all-metal body. There is an interesting anecdote connected to these bodies. It is reputed that a certain Scottish firemaster would have nothing to

FFK 350 of Worcestershire Fire Brigade is somewhat unusual in being based on a Leyland Comet chassis, with all the shortcomings that having a bonneted vehicle means. (*HCB-Angus Archive*)

UUO 305, s208, built for Devon Fire Brigade, is again a bonneted appliance, the Dodge 123, which was a short-lived choice of chassis. Notice no paint finish on the body and the light, portable pump carried above the main pump. (*HCB-Angus Archive*)

JFW 405, one of the very first Bedford S-based appliances, was built for Lindsey Fire Brigade to comply with the then-new JCDD specification for a type B water tender. The pump, 'salvaged' from a wartime trailer pump, was driven by way of a Prestage Engineering power take-off from the main engine. (*HCB-Angus Archive*)

HST13, s136, was one of a number of hose reel tenders built for the Northern Area of Scotland Fire Brigade on the Bedford A3 chassis. The semi-forward control construction was an interim conversion in anticipation of HCB Engineering's own full forward control version. (*HCB-Angus Archive*)

do with 'new fangled pop rivets' and insisted that his new all-metal appliances should be held together with set screws and nuts; HCB duly obliged and the order was placed. HCB, however, did not produce standard vehicles and there were many variants to these basic vehicles. The JCDD specification was sufficiently flexible to allow chief fire officers considerable leeway in their requirements – which the company was only too pleased to satisfy. It was, therefore, quite hard to get two identical vehicles side by side! This was to be a feature of HCB's production right up until the end in 1994.

The forward control appliances, particularly the Bedfords, came in all sizes and configurations, from the little TJ1 with sliding doors (even odd-sided door arrangements) right up to the escape carriers on the TJ7 chassis.

The Bedfords were to provide the mainstay of production right through the 1950s – the two body versions on the smaller chassis and the S type, which were all of composite construction (and to a lesser extent its 4x4 brother the R type, announced in 1953). The first R-type Bedford to be used was s325, a water tender for the Isle of Ely Fire Brigade registered GJE 904. Following behind were the Dodge-chassied versions of the lighter water tender appliances mentioned above, though in much smaller numbers, and Commer-based appliances. These appliances could be had in full or part paint – the use of stucco-finish, untreated aluminium sheet was becoming popular as a cost and maintenance saving idea.

Not all appliances were pumping based. A trio of emergency tenders was constructed, one very early for Croydon, s79, registered LOY 999, another for Bradford, s119, registered KKW 600, and a third for Rochdale Fire Brigade, s160, registered MDK 234

There were notable 'interlopers' to this Bedford/Dodge/Commer trio. One was the Austin FF, used as an appliance base for the Scottish Western Area Fire Brigade, for which five hose reel tenders and a foam tender were constructed. Another was the production of an appliance built on a Karrier Gamecock chassis, s460, registered MST 500. This appliance saw service with the Scottish Northern Area Fire Brigade. A very strange appliance was built specially for Staffordshire Fire Brigade. HCB's engineering side had won a contract from Staffordshire Fire Brigade to convert a number of Thornycroft Nubian 4x4 water tenders from the Type A specification to the Type B specification, engineering a drive to the rear and installing a Dennis No. 2 pump. This work was so successful that Staffordshire asked the company to build another from scratch. The result was Thornycroft Nubian s563, registered 6741 RF. These Nubian water tenders were ponderous vehicles to say the least. Powered by the Rolls Royce B81 petrol engine, they were lucky to manage 2 or 3 miles per gallon when on a shout.

During the 1950s there were some curious appliance configurations. There was the basic water tender, which carried 400 gallons of water, a 500 gpm pump and a 35-foot trussed ladder; and there was the pump escape with a 300-gallon tank, 500 gpm pump and a 50-foot escape. However, some interesting mix-and-match appliances fitted with a 400-gallon tank were able to run as either a pump or pump escape. A valve on the tank ensured that both escape and the full 400 gallons could not be carried, thus preventing the vehicle going overweight. And there were those that carried both a 50-foot escape and a 35-foot trussed ladder with 300 gallons of water or those that

The prototype all-metal Bedford TJ. This is distinguishable from the earlier C and D type appliances by the 'notch' in the headboard for the bell mounting. The use of fibreglass for these appliance scuttles was innovative at the time. (*HCB-Angus Archive*)

283 LTD, s511, was one of a dozen in this order contracted for the Lancashire Fire Brigade. While using the same forward control conversion as the all-metal appliance, this version was in traditional timber and sheet metal fabrication. Incidentally, both versions could be had on a Commer chassis, similarly converted. (*HCB-Angus Archive*)

9913 BH, s836, was one of a number of these diminutive appliances built on the Bedford J chassis. Having no crew doors as such, there was but one door each side, the configuration of which changed from appliance to appliance as specification dictated. They had only a 200-gallon tank rather than the 400-gallon fitted to the full-size appliances. (*HCB-Angus Archive*)

800 FFK, s588, was built as a 4x4 Bedford RL; note the chrome surround to the grill – sign of a later model, for the Worcestershire Fire Brigade. Other than its 4x4 capability, it was to standard water tender specification. (*HCB-Angus Archive*)

Again for Lindsey Fire Brigade, RBE 888, s310, was on the Bedford chassis, but with a slightly unusual locker arrangement. HCB Engineering did not offer 'stock' appliances but varied all orders to meet the needs of the brigade concerned. (*HCB-Angus Archive*)

An unregistered Commer for Kent Fire Brigade standing in the yard at Totton prior to delivery. Note the alloy ladder, nicknamed 'gut buster' by the firemen of the day due to its weight. Kent was the first brigade to do away with timber ladders. (*HCB-Angus Archive*)

Built for Croydon Fire Brigade, LOY 999, s79, was the first emergency tender built by HCB Engineering, again on an early Bedford S chassis. (*HCB-Angus Archive*)

6741 RF, s563, was a totally unique appliance, being the only Nubian-based domestic appliance built by HCB-Angus. It was built for Staffordshire Fire Brigade as an 'extra' appliance to match the number of Carmichael-built appliances that HCB Engineering had converted from A to B water tender specification. (*HCB-Angus Archive*)

carried either a 50-foot escape or a portable pump over the pump bay; just about any configuration, HCB made them all!

HCB were also working on a light appliance based on the Land Rover chassis but were having considerable difficulty with the Rover Company, which was not being co-operative in giving factory approval to the conversion. In the end the company went ahead with production anyway and Land Rover approval came later. This did mean, of course, that early users were not mainstream brigades but were industrial companies looking for a light fire appliance. The first was ordered in the early part of 1960 and was delivered shortly after. This was actually a rescue tender for Guernsey Airport, s599. The first pumping appliance built on a Land Rover was for Short Brothers, Belfast, s767, registered 5239 EZ.

HCB Engineering had been attempting to get type approval from the Rover Car Company for a fire appliance conversion but that company had been dragging its heels so HCB-Angus just built one anyway! This was the first pumping appliance, s769, registered 5239 EZ, built for Short Brothers & Harland (Belfast). (*HCB-Angus Archive*)

5
The 1960s

The announcement by Bedford in 1960 of the TK series, replacement for the S type (then nearly ten years old), enabled HCB to move things along somewhat and the first TK-based appliance went on the run in 1961 with Merionethshire Fire Brigade. This was s566, registered EFF 108. While the Bedford product had a full-width curved windscreen, the company replaced this with a two-piece flat glass screen; it rebuilt the cab from the scuttle waistline upward. Though there were two screens, HCB was applying a 'wider and deeper' policy to windscreen provision, first seen on the forward control vehicles. It was to be nearly ten years before this was revised and replaced with a larger curved glass screen (from an AEC lorry design). Meanwhile, the smaller Bedfords continued to be built in numbers – in both composite and all-metal formats.

The 1960s brought with it the change of name to HCB-Angus, as noted in the company history, and with it a worldwide market and expansion into other chassis and appliance types. Inspection and examination of the company's practices led to accreditation with the UK government, thus allowing tendering for, and winning UK ministry and military contracts.

The first of these were for a number of rescue tenders built for the Ministry of Transport and Civil Aviation based on the Bedford R short wheelbase chassis. While not carrying a pump or water, they carried a comprehensive kit of penetration gear aimed at getting crews out of aircraft in the shortest possible time. The first batch of six was ordered in 1959, s883 – s889, registered VXN 530 – 536. There were many problems with the kit for these appliances and delivery did not take place until late in 1960. More followed over the next few years.

The first order for the Ministry of Defence was for some water/foam tenders for the Admiralty on Bedford R long wheelbase chassis. These had an elliptical tank that was built by Longwell Green in Bristol. This became established practice; if it had an elliptical tank, Longwell Green almost certainly built it as a sub-contract, a practice that continued until that company went into receivership in 1992. These appliances were s833 – s839, registered 13 RN 13 – 19, and carried 900 gallons of water and 30 of foam compound. As before, this initial batch was followed by repeat orders over the next few years.

VXN 877, s530, was one of a number of these Bedford RL-based ETs built for the Ministry of Transport and Civil Aviation over a period of years. HCB Engineering had problems kitting these appliances as the specification called for a high-cycle circular saw for cutting into fuselages. These proved very difficult to obtain and this delayed the early appliances for some time. This appliance served at Stanstead. (*HCB-Angus Archive*)

The Admiralty ordered a number of these foam tenders (some carried ladder racks), carrying 900 gallons of water and 30 gallons of foam compound. This one, s885, registered 13RN15, is pictured in the works yard awaiting delivery. (*HCB-Angus Archive*)

The 1960s

TAW 543, s479, for Shropshire Fire Brigade was one of a pair described as 'multi-purpose' – that is they carried everything: 400 gallons of water, a main pump, a light portable pump, 30-foot ladder and a 45-foot escape. This all-up weight must have given the petrol-engined Bedford quite a load! (*HCB-Angus Archive*)

While the design staff and workshops had been busy with the design and construction of vehicles on many different chassis, the technical department had also been busy. New designs for PTOs were required, not only with different ratios to suit the new chassis being taken on board but also of the driveline variety where this was more suitable. However, the most innovative design task was the development of the company's own fire pump. Fire pumps in general use at the time for water tenders answered the basic requirement for 500 gallons of water per minute at 100 psi and if higher pressures were need for hose reel fog guns, then this was provided by a secondary pump.

The company decided, however, that they would aim for a single pump that could do both duties without the need for the booster element - a dual pressure pump.

The design specification dated seventh of June 1961 called for -

Main duty: 500 gpm at 100 psi at 2,750 pump rpm
High-Pressure duty: 80–100 gpm at 330 psi at 4,500 pump rpm

The change over from main duty to high-pressure duty was achieved merely by increasing pump rpm. An interceptor valve prevented the high-pressure water from entering the main hose lines – which could not stand up to that pressure, needless to say!

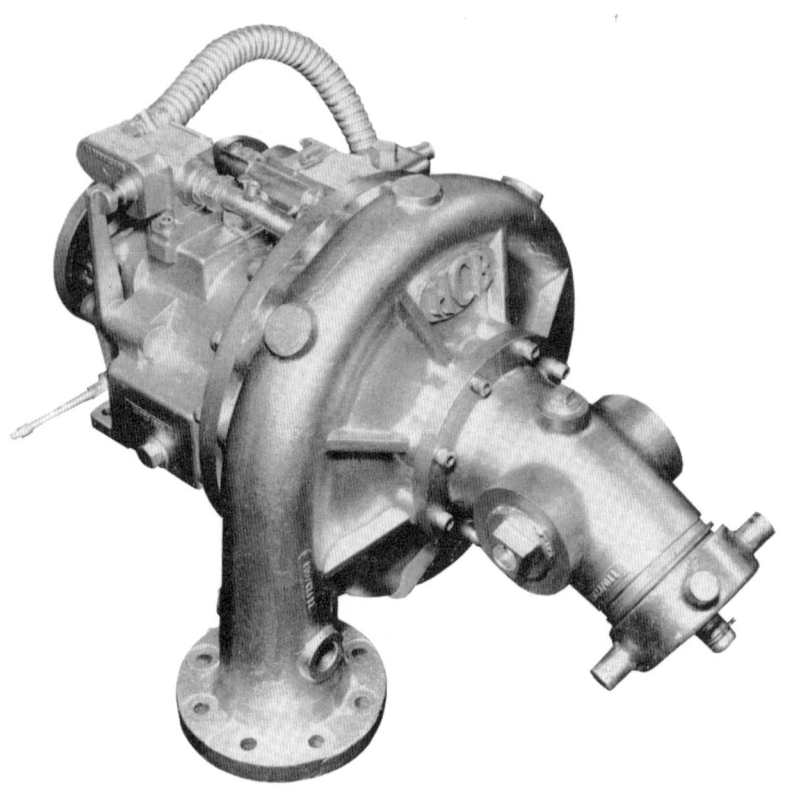

The basic body of the HCB Angus pump. Designed and built as a multi-purpose low/high-pressure pump (pressure change was just by an increase in revs plus an interceptor valve to prevent over-pressure in the main delivery). The pump worked well when all was right but was beset with mechanical problems that were never truly resolved. All the external 'bits' to the pump were by Trinity, as with most pump builders. (*HCB-Angus Archive*)

The design and manufacture of the pump was entrusted to J. & S. Pumps Ltd of Surrey. They quickly designed and produced the prototype and this was first run on the first of May 1962, driven by the Bedford 300 cubic inch petrol engine, the usual appliance power plant at the time. There were problems at first and the duties were not carried out. There were several mechanical problems and the pump could not meet the specification requirements with the power available from the engine. However, these problems were eventually overcome (though the problems with the mechanical water seal to the drive spindle, which allowed water to leak away, were never really resolved and were the cause of many brigade complaints). The pump finally made it into production in July 1962 in its Mark 1 form and many were supplied to brigades all round the world until 1967. Unfortunately, the company did not patent the design work for the pump and Godiva announced a very similar pump in August of 1965. Given the problems that the HCB-Angus pump was giving, it is not surprising that sales were lost to the competition. Subsequently, the company revised the whole pump design and in 1966 the Mark 2 pump was commissioned from SACO Pumps and entered production in 1967 without the problems of its predecessor. However, Godiva announced a new pump just one year later, which could pump at high and low pressure simultaneously. Orders for the HCB-Angus pump dried up almost instantly and production was called to a halt late in 1968. In all, approximately 150 pumps were built, perhaps not the production rate that the company had hoped for but an interesting period.

LEN 999, an early Bedford TK built as s609, for Bury Fire Brigade. Note that HCB replaced the one-piece Bedford screen with two flat glasses (the same glass as in the TJ conversions). The overall effect was claimed to give sight lines 'deeper and wider' than standard. (*HCB-Angus Archive*)

Built for the Ministry of Public Buildings and Works, Bedford TK s2015, registered ALT 468H, is seen here running as an escape carrier. (*HCB-Angus Archive*)

The first pair of Land Rover forward control chassis to be converted for fire fighting purposes by the company were s829/830, registered 290 and 291 GAC being built for Warwickshire Fire Brigade. They did not have an engine driven pump as later versions did but had a 100 gallon tank supplying a light portable pump. Here we see one of the pair at its handing over ceremony. (*HCB-Angus Archive*)

By the late 1960s the Bedford TK with the 300 cubic inch petrol engine was very much the preferred base for HCB-Angus production of water tenders but it was regarded by some to be underpowered, especially as vehicle weights were increasing due to the amount of small gear being carried. In order to address this, HCB-Angus offered a number of options. Their most original was to give the Bedford engine to Janspeed Ltd for them to up-rate. This was done with Bedford's approval and involved machining 1/8 inch from the cylinder head, manufacturing a new inlet manifold to accommodate a pair of Stromberg carburettors (as fitted to the Triumph TR4), and constructing a free breathing multi-pipe exhaust system. This provided a useful lift to both the maximum horsepower and to the engine torque but did nothing for the fuel consumption.

There followed two alternatives. The first of these was to fit the Jaguar XK engine in place of the Bedford. Many manufacturers frequently used this 4.2 litre twin overhead camshaft engine as a light, alternative power source. It was, for instance, used in the Scorpion light tank and HCB-Angus decided to use it, as it provided a power increase with no weight disadvantage. While it did the job and drove well, the installation was flawed and the engines suffered greatly from cracked cylinder blocks and heads due to under-cooling. Many appliances spent periods of time off the run while remedies were sought. The best of these seemed to be the mounting of a large scoop under the front bumper to direct air, not so much through the radiator as around the engine itself, and this seemed to do the trick. That said, most if not all of the Jaguar-engined appliances underwent an engine replacement, usually with a Perkins diesel unit.

The second alternative engine was the Rolls Royce B61 petrol engine. Again, a favourite with the military, it did not draw a great deal of interest from UK brigades and was installed in very few appliances.

In attempt to obtain more power for the Bedford range at the time when petrol engines reigned supreme, HCB Angus offered three options. One, seen on the left, was to have Janspeed Conversions work on the engine. Twin Stromberg carburettors, special inlet and exhaust manifold and a planed head gave a good increase in power; the second, seen on the right, was to fit the Jaguar XK 4.2 engine. This was not a success as there were great cooling issues resulting in many cracked engines. The third, not seen here, was to fit the Rolls Royce B61 engine, which, though expensive, was reliable. (*HCB-Angus Archive*)

As time went on, diesels became more popular; their suitability for fire appliances had always been a problem due to the fact that they were slow revving and not quick to respond, but this was changing as diesels developed and they began to be the chassis makers' fitment of choice. The use of petrol engines was soon put aside as the diesel came to reign supreme.

The 1960s, as mentioned earlier, was an expansive time for the company. The involvement with Angus Fire broadened its customer base and increased experience resulted in the building of other appliance designs and the adoption of alternative chassis, not always governed by UK legislation and standards. For instance, weight restrictions on UK roads do not apply in many other countries, particularly in the Third World, allowing much heavier vehicle weights on the same base chassis. On the home front, the Bedford TJ and TK series chassis continued to provide the vast majority of appliance bases but there were some notable others, both for home and for non-UK appliances.

The problems that the company had in gaining Rover Company approval for its fire appliance conversions have been mentioned earlier but once permission was obtained, work started in earnest. By the end of the decade, Land Rover-based appliances produced by the company were in use in over twenty countries; after all the Land Rover brand was already world famous, so people bought with confidence. A ground breaking development in 1964 saw Warwickshire Fire Brigade take on the first forward control Land Rovers, s829/830, registered 291/292 GAC. These were specified with a 150-gallon water capacity but were eventually completed with a 100-gallon tank. This was due to the problems the company had with the total all-up weight of the vehicles and the consequent overloading of the front axle, however much the redesign work moved the tank to the rear. The vehicles did eventually enter service and the hard work the company had put into their design and construction did, indeed, pay off when they tendered for and received orders from the Ministry of Defence for similar vehicles in various batches (one for forty-one vehicles, s5166.1 – 41) over the next ten years or so. The forward control chassis had appliances built on it for various counties around the world, such as five dry powder units for South Africa, s1772 – 1776, and a trio of similar vehicles for Syria, s2330 – 2332.

The first of the AEC chassis to be used was s789, registered 3982 RU, an emergency tender for Bournemouth Fire Brigade, closely followed by a pair of Snorkel appliances, s877, registered 209 HAT, for Hull Fire Brigade and s878, registered BAD 659B, for Gloucestershire Fire Brigade. The first pumping appliance was s880, registered ATN 366B, for Newcastle upon Tyne. Several more followed during the decade, including a water carrier for Nottingham City Fire Brigade, s1334, registered LTV 99F, and a pump escape, s1673, registered MFR 164G, for Blackpool Fire Brigade.

Another new chassis to be used during the 1960s was the ERF 84RS, chosen as the need for heavier chassis was acknowledged. The first of these was to provide the base for a Simon Snorkel, s1306, registered EFE 579E, for Lincoln City Fire Brigade, followed shortly after by a pumping appliance for Newcastle and Gateshead Fire Brigade, s1432, registered LBB 913D. An interesting trio among the ERFs are those registered SMH 346F, 347F, and 348F, s1577–9, for the London Fire Brigade as dual-

s880 is an early appliance built on an AEC chassis. Registered ATN336B, it was built to an order for Fire Armour, who had just joined up with HCB Engineering to become HCB-Angus, for Newcastle and Gateshead Fire Brigade. What this black and white photograph does not do justice to is the maroon and red livery this brigade used for its machines. (*HCB-Angus Archive*)

SMH 347F, s1578, was the second of a trio of ERF appliances built for London Fire Brigade. Usually running with a London-pattern wooden escape mounted up top, they frequently ran as water tenders just with a 35-foot trussed ladder mounted as here. A large machine, these ERFs are thought by many to be the last of the 'real' fire engines! (*HCB-Angus Archive*)

Seen here at the ERF works, HCB Angus, in conjunction with Jennings and ERF, worked to produce a double cab with the minimum of development – by using the same door mouldings back to back. All these cab mouldings were produced by Jennings and supplied to the various end users. (*HCB-Angus Archive*)

purpose appliances. HCB-Angus had never tendered for London appliances before, found it difficult to reach the standards required by that brigade, and did not tender again for pumping appliances for some 15 years. The ERF chassis, with its distinctive end-to-end cab (two cabs joined back-to-back to create the crew cab), was developed by Jennings (coachbuilders of Sandbach and a branch of ERF) and HCB-Angus as a joint program, though all cabs were built by Jennings and were bought in by HCB-Angus. The majority of ERF appliances built were for hydraulic platform (booms alone) or pump hydraulic platform use (booms plus an integral fire pump supplying the top of the booms), though a reasonable number of water tender and pump escape appliances were also built. These were thought by many to be the most elegant of fire appliances built in the UK, not only then, but also for all time. The chassis had only a relatively short utilisation time – the first appearing in 1966 and the last leaving the works in 1972. South Africa was to purchase twenty-three pump hydraulic platform appliances in one order (s1887 – s1910). What was neither understood nor apparent was that some of these appliances, once landed in South Africa, were driven straight through to Rhodesia, which at the time was subject to an embargo by the UK government due to Ian Smith's Unilateral Declaration of Independence in 1965. The British government had imposed a trade embargo when the Smith administration had declared the British colony independent rather than be subject to a majority black government as a result of normal independence from the Crown. 'Sanctions busting', I believe it was called!

At the other end of the weight scale, the company had made some inroads into the lightweight range with Land Rover-based appliances, but they were small vehicles and lacked the space required to stow much small gear. The introduction by the Ford Motor Co. in October of 1962 of that ubiquitous vehicle the Ford Transit changed this. HCB-Angus saw the opportunity for a light fire appliance and quickly devised a driveline PTO to bring a drive up behind the gearbox into the cargo space. This enabled a vehicle engine-driven pump to be carried within the body with the water tank, together with ample shuttered small gear rack space. Externally there were various options, such as the rear door being top hinged or removed altogether. Together with the side-opening door option, various configurations of stowage were possible. Courtauds Engineering was the first to purchase a Transit-based appliance with s1445, registered GBE 265E. It carried 60 gallons of water to supply its vehicle engine-driven pump. During the remainder of the decade approximately a dozen such appliances were built, mostly for industrial brigades, including several for the Ford Motor Co.; Monaghan Fire Brigade took delivery of three, s155 – s157, registered EBI 271, 588 and 589.

Further expansion in terms of design and construction came with the development of full-sized airfield crash tenders, almost universally, at this time, based on the Thornycroft Nubian 6x6 chassis and, to a lesser extent, the Bedford RL. HCB-Angus started its involvement at this heavy end of the market with two appliances for BAC Bristol, s800, registered 28 RHY, and s818, registered 289 RHY, during 1962/63. This, again, saw the start of worldwide demand and many appliances were shipped abroad during the ensuing years.

An odd little trio of vehicles was constructed in the mid-1960s based on the Austin/Morris FG 40, whose cab with the 'angle plan' cab doors made them so distinctive, angled so that when opened they still did not protrude beyond the width of the vehicle. They were full pumping appliances, carrying 125-gallon tanks and a vehicle engine-driven pump. Though mechanically the same, all three were slightly different in body, with changes in locker provision and ladder carrying ability. In particular, the J. S. Fry vehicle had to have a severely troughed roofline as the garage it was to go in was in fact built with a Land Rover fire engine in mind. The three vehicles were: s872, registered LSB 149, for the Western Area Fire Brigade in Scotland; s1031, registered BAA 778C, for J. S. Fry Ltd (Bristol); and s1415, registered FIO 123, for County Kildare Fire Brigade, Ireland.

This decade saw the last of the orders emanating from Kent Fire Brigade for their unique specification water tender appliances. There were four batches during the decade: s1270 – s1282, based on the Commer VAKS741; s1498 – s1509 on the Commer VBKW 741; s1658 – s1669 on the Commer VCKW 741; and, lastly, s2021 – s2038, also on the Commer VCKS 741.

The Ford D series was first used by HCB-Angus when Gloucestershire Fire Service ordered six pumping appliances, s1457 – s1462, registered LDG 219F to 296F. There were many more to come.

During this decade most orders had been for no more than five or six appliances per year per brigade, an exception being Kent, as outlined above. Even orders for overseas, frequently via the Crown Agency, were for four or five vehicles bound for a

Above: The announcement by the Ford Motor Company of the Transit van took the light commercial fraternity by storm and it was not long before HCB-Angus had not only produced an appliance but had developed a drive line PTO to bring the drive up through the van floor to drive a Godiva pump. This prototype being s1445, registered GBE 265E, belonged to Courtauds Engineering. (*HCB-Angus Archive*)

Left: A rear view of the Transit. The water tank can be seen across the width of the van behind the pump, the drive coming up through the floor behind the gearbox and having a carden shaft to drive to the pump at the rear. (*HCB-Angus Archive*)

This version, built for the Ford Motor Co. and not yet painted, did away with the rear door completely, and did not have a PTO drive but instead used a self-contained, light, portable pump that was mounted on a slide-out cradle. It could draw water from an onboard tank by way of a flexible hose. This vehicle was for internal duties so was not registered and was built on s1632. (*HCB-Angus Archive*)

The Thornycroft Nubian formed the basis for many and varied airfield crash tenders. This one, s1532, was one of a group of eight built for West Pakistan and carried the legend 'Do not park this vehicle in full sun', no doubt aware of the pressurised carbon dioxide bottles on board! (*HCB-Angus Archive*)

These diminutive appliances (two groups of two) built on Bedford TJ1 pick-ups were also for Pakistan, the eastern side this time. They were towing vehicles, having no vehicle engine-driven pump but carrying a light portable pump for external use plus fire fighting kit. This one is s1246. (*HCB-Angus Archive*)

While the Austin/Morris FG chassis had been used a number of times as a hose reel tender, this appliance and its two brothers were the only three built as full pumps. This one, s1031, registered BAA 778C, was for J. S. Fry & Sons' chocolate factory in Bristol and is now in the ownership of the author. They carried 125 gallons of water and have a vehicle engine-driven Godiva FWPS pump. (*HCB-Angus Archive*)

single destination. As time went on, these orders became more frequent and for more diverse destinations. An exception to this, which no doubt kept the accountants happy, was a single order for forty-five Bedford RL-based water tenders, s1150 – s1195, for Malaysia. This must have been the nearest HCB-Angus had got to mass production!

Before moving on to the next decade, there a few odd vehicles that deserve a mention – some not strictly fire appliances.

The first of these was the first combined aerial pumping appliance that HCB-Angus built, which was delivered to Ceylon Fire Service on a Bedford TK chassis (s854), known in those days as a pump hydraulic platform. This enabled a Simon Snorkel appliance, a 65-foot version, to drive its own fire pump without the need for a support appliance to provide the water and pump. The file shows many pages of arithmetic as the engineers devised two suitable power take offs, one to drive the hydraulics and the other to drive the water pump. In all, some 136 Simon Snorkel-based appliances were built and were delivered to brigades all over the world.

The Chilean Oil Refinery Company ordered a pair of foam tenders, s1063 and s1064, on Leyland Comet chassis with the LAD cab. Unique in design, they resembled American vehicles as all the kit was hung on the outside rather than being fitted within lockers. One of these vehicles was the subject of a great deal of argument when the pump burst on its first test once on site. To cut a long story short, it turned out that the pump had been run up to maximum speed against closed deliveries while fed from a hydrant – all well and good, except that the refinery water mains were already at 150 psi pressure! However, they must have been good in service, as they were not replaced until some fifteen years later by a pair of Ford D series refinery tenders, s5167.1 – 2.

Manchester Fire Brigade commissioned HCB-Angus to build three pump escape appliances based on Albion CH13EL chassis, s1719 – s1722, registered JVU 593F – 595F. These were the only three Albion-based pumping appliances built for a UK brigade by the company.

Durham Fire Brigade ordered a Bedford RL, s675, registered 6567 PT, as a breakdown vehicle; it remained in service for many years before finding a second life with a local garage. An almost identical vehicle was built shortly after for the Lindsey (Lincolnshire) Fire Brigade, s1043, registered BBE 739B.

The last to mention in this decade are a group of water cannon used for riot suppression in their respective countries. Obviously a fire appliance has the makings of a good water cannon: a built-in water supply, a pump, and with HCB-Angus's sandwich PTO giving the ability to pump on the move. During the 1960s four groups of these vehicles were built, all on Bedfords but all on different chassis models. The first pair, s1112 and s1113, was for the Libyan government and was built on Bedford KF chassis; the second group, s1373 – s1382, for South Africa on the RL chassis; the third for Saudi Arabia, s1489 and s1490, on Bedford J5 with an unusual 4x4 conversion; and the last for Kuwait on the Bedford TKG, s2086 and s2087.

As crowd control units they were plumbed a little differently from fire appliances – they were fitted with cannon at high level with remote control from within a protected turret and were fitted with drenching sprays to flush water down all sides of the vehicle for fire or chemical suppression while they were seeing action.

Looking very American in style, this Leyland Comet-based refinery vehicle was one of a pair built for the Chilean Oil Company under s1063 and 4. (*HCB-Angus Archive*)

6567 PT, s675, was a Bedford RL-based breakdown truck built for Durham County Fire Brigade. The company built three breakdown trucks in all, harking back to their commercial body building days. (*HCB-Angus Archive*)

Riot trucks, while not exactly being fire-fighting vehicles, need a pump-driven water supply. This Bedford RL-based version, S1373, one of an order for ten, was built for South Africa. Several other Middle and Far Eastern countries bought similar vehicles. (*HCB-Angus Archive*)

The announcement of the Ford D series of tilt cab trucks opened up some stiff competition to the Bedfords. Here we see one of the forty that Greater Manchester Fire Service ordered awaiting its registration. (*HCB-Angus Archive*)

A similarly large order was placed by Lancashire Fire Brigade, several vehicles of which order eventually ended up with Manchester following a re-organisation. Here are some clogging up the yard awaiting delivery. (*HCB-Angus Archive*)

GPX 70N, being Leyland 16BT s5127, would have been an oddity in the Hampshire Fire Brigade. However, it should never have been there as the original order came from India but when the time came, the deal fell through. Hampshire therefore got themselves a Pump Hydraulic Platform with 70-foot booms for a bargain price. (*HCB-Angus Archive*)

In the company's terminology this is a T10: a fully cabbed water tender but with a 1,000-gallon tank. This order for Nigeria was for nine appliances on s5646.1–9. (*HCB-Angus Archive*)

6
The 1970s

The 1970s were busy days for HCB-Angus. On the home front, vehicle weight and power were on the increase, together with the move towards diesel engines. Production for the rest of the world was running at record levels. As related earlier, the Bedford TKG series was being offered with upgraded petrol engines and the Bedford diesel was becoming more popular. The Bedford TJs were coming to the end of their lives as a chassis of choice; they were just no longer tough enough. Replacing them were two newcomers to the scene: the Dodge K and Ford D vehicles. These did not receive the high degree of cab makeover that HCB-Angus had bestowed on the Bedfords; as they were tilt cabs, they had to remain as they came from the manufacturer.

The decade got off to an interesting start; Simon Engineering had placed a pair of orders with HCB-Angus for the fire engineering and bodying of a pair of Leyland 16 BT appliances, one as a hydraulic platform and the other as a pump hydraulic platform. The PHP, s5126, duly went to Nova Sad, Yugoslavia, but the HP that was due to go to India was left in the company's yard when negotiations with the customer failed. Hampshire Fire Brigade, with their headquarters just down the road from HCB-Angus, heard about it and ended up with a bargain! The Leyland was registered GPX 70N, s5127.

There were some very significant developments on the technical front, however. The use of diesel engines had become almost universal but a further technical development gained general acceptance within a very short time. In 1973 HCB-Angus announced its first automatic transmission fire appliance, s5414, a Dodge K850 powered by a Perkins V8 diesel engine and fitted with an Allison fully automatic gearbox. HCB-Angus had to produce yet another version of its sandwich power take off to mate these two together. The appliance travelled around the country as a demonstrator and it is not known where this appliance eventually saw service. By the end of the decade, the use of diesel engines and auto boxes as a fitment to appliances was widespread.

In the late 1960s HCB-Angus had responded to a Ministry of Defence design specification for a replacement vehicle for the now aging fleet of airfield first strike vehicles based on Land Rovers. What was required was an updated and upgraded machine designed to be first on scene in the event of a crash or suchlike incident. At the same time, both the Fleet Air Arm of the Royal Navy and the Army Air Corps were looking for a similar vehicle. Out of this MoD requirement the Truck, Airfield Crash Rescue (TACR) was born.

The TACR1 was intended for use as a rapid intervention vehicle (RIV) on all RAF and FAA air stations around the world during the 1970s and into the 1980s. According to official publications of the time, the TACR was to fulfil several main functions: the rescue of aircrew from crashed aircraft; extinguishing of small aircraft fires; and in addition, the truck could be used for escorting aircraft as a precautionary measure against starting and taxiing fire hazards.

The TACR was designed to accommodate a crew of three, two in the cab with the third on a rear facing seat at the back of the vehicle – not the most pleasant of rides. Small gear and 100 gallons of premixed foam were carried. Air portability by the Hercules transport aircraft just coming into service with the RAF was required. The chassis was a Land Rover 109-inch wheelbase model complete with cab and the following options:

a) Centre Power take off
b) Strengthened axles
c) Two seats only in the cab (as apposed to the normal three)
d) Inertia safety belts
e) Heavy-duty springs
f) 9.00 x 16 Tyres and wheels
g) Heavy-duty battery

In all, HCB-Angus built ninety-two of these appliances between 1970 and 1979, initially on the Series 2a one-ton Land Rover but latterly on the Series 3. Interestingly, they came with the four-cylinder engine rather than the six, as fitted to the one-ton civilian version. This was to maintain compatibility with the other Land Rovers in service with the MoD and thus aid spares and service requirements. However, this must not have done a great deal for the performance of a vehicle that was running very close to the chassis manufacturer's all-up weight. This was a very capable vehicle and many have survived well beyond their service life.

They were ordered in a number of batches:

s2513 – s2529: Ministry of Technology, RAF, September 1970
s5004.1 – 5: Ministry of Technology, Army, August 1980
s5044.1 – 14: Ministry of Defence, Navy, January 1971
s5264.1 – 3: Ministry of Defence, Navy, January 1971
s5363.1 – 35: Ministry of Defence, RAF, November 1972
s5528.1 – 6: Ministry of Technology, RAF, April 1973
s5566.1 – 5: Ministry of Defence, Army, August 1974
s5651.1 – 2: Ministry of Defence, February 1975
s5811.1 – 5: Ministry of Defence, Navy, July of 1976

Above: The TACR (Truck Air Craft Rescue) was developed against a very tight Ministry specification based on the Land Rover S2a chassis cab. This one, s2513, was the first of many, in this case an order for seventeen. (*HCB-Angus Archive*)

Left: The rather precarious extra seat was fitted centrally at the rear with communication with the rest of the crew being by way of speaking tube. There are many stories of the vehicle coming to a stop, the man at the back getting off and then the vehicle moving away to complete its journey. (*HCB-Angus Archive*)

Plate 1: GXM 627, a Dodge Kew from the Isle of Wight Fire Brigade. One of a group of five that first saw service with the Auxiliary Fire Service, it was sent to HCB Engineering for conversion from Type A to Type B water tender specification. It was stationed at Freshwater, Ventnor, Newport and East Cowes. (*Photographer unknown*)

Plate 2: PKN 541 is a Commer 21A, one of a batch of over twenty appliances ordered by Kent Fire Brigade in 1951 as that brigade sought to replace its fire fighting vehicles, worn out in the aftermath of the Second World War. Stationed at Teynham, when sold out of service it was converted to 4x4 configuration by Caffyns (Folkstone) and saw further service on an Lympne Airport. (*John Meakins*)

Plate 3: MBE 978, s978, was ordered by the Lindsey Fire Brigade as a towing vehicle, that is, it had no main pump but just a low-capacity pump driven from the side of the gear box, feeding a hose reel. The semi forward control conversion was not undertaken by HCB Engineering but by Neville (coachbuilders) in Southampton. Stationed originally at Caistor, it is seen here with its second user livery, the London Brick Company. (*Simon Rowley*)

Plate 4: The South Eastern Fire Brigade of Scotland was an early specifier of the Big Bedford. This pumping appliance, s199, registered NSF 200, was lightly stressed as it only carried 100 gallons of water to supply its Dennis pump. It was stationed for its entire career at Musselburgh. (*Ken Read*)

Plate 5: S770, registered 401 SFK, constructed on a Bedford J4 chassis for the Hereford & Worcester Fire Brigade, is the fully forward control chassis conversion using the fibreglass scuttle and otherwise conventional timber and metal construction. Fitted with a 400 gallon tank and a Gwynne main pump, it was stationed at Tenbury, Kidderminster and then on reserve. (*Simon Rowley*)

Plate 6: This, however, is the full metal version, s720, registered 43 EPO for the West Sussex Fire Brigade. Construction was somewhat unconventional for the day, with the vehicle having only two sliding doors for the whole crew to access the cab. Technical specification was wholly conventional, a Dennis pump being fed from a 400-gallon tank. This engine was stationed at Littlehampton for its service life. (*Author*)

Plate 7: A truly transitional appliance for HCB Angus. This vehicle was ordered from Fire Armour Ltd by Newcastle and Gateshead Fire Brigade but was built by HCB-Angus in Totton. Notice it even carries a Fire Armour logo over the radiator. S880, registered ATN 366B, wears the unique colour scheme of this brigade on its AEC-chassied body. It was stationed at City East, Gateshead and City West after re-organisation in 1974. (*Ron Henderson*)

Plate 8: The announcement by Vauxhall Motors of the TK series of lorries gave HCB a new chassis to work with. The Bedford scuttle was cut away at the windscreen base and replaced with a split screen and fibreglass construction to give a deeper and wider view. This vehicle, s1066, registered ASK 701C, for the Central Area Fire Brigade of Scotland carries, as a dual purpose appliance, everything: 50-foot escape, short and long trussed extension and roof ladders, together with 400 gallons of water and a main Godiva pump. It was stationed at Wick, and then at Lerwick after the 1974 re-organisation. (*Ken Read*)

Plate 9: HCB Engineering built only three of these Austin/Morris FG 40 pumping appliances. This one, s1031, was built for J. S. Fry Ltd, Bristol (chocolate manufacturers) and registered BAA 778C. Carrying just 100 gallons of water and equipped with a Godiva FWPS pump, this appliance is now in the ownership of the author. (*Dave Gothard*)

Plate 10: Merioneth Fire Brigade purchased one appliance per year from HCB-Angus for some years, always on a Bedford chassis. Here we have s1315, registered EFF 317D (later re-registered FEY 209D), based on a J4 chassis. This appliance, a water tender, is of traditional timber frame/metal cladding construction and was fitted with one of HCB-Angus' own pumps. It served all its career at Aberdyfi. (*Author*)

Plate 11: The 84RS chassis manufactured by ERF Ltd formed the basis for many heavier fire appliances and here we have s1542, registered NRY 999F, a pump hydraulic platform for Leicester City Fire Brigade. Seventy-foot booms were fitted, and 200 gallons of water were carried, together with an engine-driven main pump. It was stationed at Lancaster Place its entire career. (*Simon Engineering*)

Plate 12: Seen here in its second life as a civilian appliance, CVO 367J, originally 22 FG 67, s1818, and part of the first order of ten for the British Army in 1968 for light fire appliances, this Land Rover FC carried 125 gallons of water and had a Godiva FWPS pump. HCB-Angus had to overcome considerable problems with weight distribution and front axle overloading in developing these vehicles. (*Archie McKinnon*)

Plate 13: Bristol City Fire Brigade ordered this dual purpose appliance, s5078, registered BHY 748J. It is seen here at the FVRE Cobham undergoing a tilt test, as all new models of fire appliance were required to do in order to establish their stability. It carried 400 gallons of water as well as a 50-foot escape and was stationed at Speedwell. (*HCB-Angus*)

Plate 14: The TACR was conceived and built by HCB-Angus as a response to a Ministry of Defence proposal. On display here is the first of the Land Rover Series 3 versions for the Navy. The appliance was s5651.1, registered 91 RN 48, and is seen here in red although others of the series were painted drab NATO green. (*HCB-Angus*)

Plate 15: S 1177, registration UFV 400K, was ordered by Blackpool Fire Brigade and is seen here outside Albert Road Fire Station. An unusual specification for an emergency tender, it had an engine-driven pump fed from a 200-gallon tank as well as the more usual electrically powered rescue equipment associated with ETs. It also carried a full crew of six. Notice that the appliance does not carry the HCB-Angus badge as the chief fire officer of the day would not allow body builder plates to be applied to any of his vehicles. (*Ron Henderson*)

Plate 16: Cumberland Fire Service, one of the country's smaller country brigades, ordered this Ford D 1070-chassied pump hydraulic platform on s1185, registered DRM 620K. It had 50-foot Simon Snorkel booms and had an engine-driven Godiva pump. It is seen here after 1974, when Cumbria had been created. It was stationed at Workington and then used as a reserve. (*Andy Anderson*)

Plate 17: Gloucestershire Fire and Rescue Service ordered a group of four Ford D series-based appliances in 1973 on s5362.1–4, registered PDF 829M – 832M. They were built as water tender ladders on the D 1013 chassis. (*Photographer unknown*)

Plate 18: The scuttle on this Bedford TK was first developed to be fitted to the Unipower Invader crash tender but the company tried it on some of the Bedfords. This water tender ladder was constructed for Coventry Fire Service in 1973 on s5355, registered PHP 31M. It was one of the few appliances to be fitted with the Rolls Royce B61 engine, offered as an alternative to the Bedford power plant. The appliance is seen here in its post-re-organisation West Midland Fire Service livery. (*Simon Rowley*)

Plate 19: British Hovercraft (Scilly Isles) contracted the construction of this light crash tender on a Dodge W400 chassis. It was, in fact, bodied by Longwell Green of Bristol as a sub-contract on s5813, registered JHO 555S. The vehicle carried 220 gallons of pre-mix foam compound. It was the prototype of the Dodge W400 that inspired the Corgi model. (*HCB-Angus*)

Plate 20: In 1976, HCB-Angus developed the Commer G11 Commando chassis for fire appliance use. The result was demonstrator s5491, eventually registered LRX 721P. The appliance spent its entire service life with the UKAEA at the Harwell establishment before entering preservation. (*Author*)

Plate 27: This is one of a pair of Bedford M chassis built for the Sultanate of Oman on s6151.1–2. They were built as normal water tender ladders so just why the camouflage paint finish has been applied is not clear. (*HCB-Angus*)

Plate 28: One of the pair of Thornycroft Nubian Super Major crash tenders supplied to Dubai Airport during 1980 on s6023.1–2. Though wearing Thornycroft badges, they were at this time now part of Scammell Motors, in turn part of the Leyland Group. (*HCB-Angus*)

Plate 25: When delivery was urgent, Heavy Lift Cargo Airlines (Australia) were contracted for delivery. This staged photograph shows a cargo of various appliances awaiting delivery to the Middle East. (*HCB-Angus*)

Plate 26: When is a CSV not a CSV? When it's one of these. This lookalike was only offered to non-UK customers and was a conventional build system with the CSV skins applied. (*HCB-Angus*)

Plate 23: Resting in the evening sun is a Land Rover S3 of unknown identity, other than the supposition that it is going abroad, having a tropical cab roof and left-hand drive. It is fitted with the HCB-Angus development the 'fish fryer' top-hinged equipment bins rather than conventional lockers. The system worked well, the gas strut-suspended lids opening to give easy access to the equipment inside. (*HCB-Angus*)

Plate 24: The Crew Safety Vehicle was probably the major technical development from HCB-Angus during their manufacturing lifetime. Shown here is an Isle of Wight Fire Brigade appliance, JDL 999W, one of a pair ordered in 1977 on s6020.1–2 and delivered in this white livery, a colour that suited these appliances. It was stationed at Newport, Yarmouth and Sandown. (*HCB-Angus*)

Plate 21: Cork County Fire Service placed an order for four of the many hundreds of Bedford TK water tender ladder appliances built over the years. Ordered in 1977 on s5746.1–4 and registered 6939 – 6942 ZT, they were a little unusual for the time in having an illuminated 'FIRE' sign over the windscreen. (*HCB-Angus*)

Plate 22: A pair of water carriers for the Kingdom of Bahrain built on s5941.1–2 on the heavy-duty Bedford KH chassis. They carried 2,000 gallons of water and had a Godiva pump. The white paint was presumably some limited protection against heat gain by the water. (*HCB-Angus*)

Plate 29: S6392.1–3 were built on an order from the Nigerian National Petroleum Company. The Bedford M chassis with sand tyres was specified, fitted with a 500-gallon foam tank, seven hand lines and an Angus FWM1800 foam canon fed from a Godiva UFPX pump. Interestingly, no water was carried. (*HCB-Angus*)

Plate 30: Oxfordshire Fire and Rescue Service ordered their first Volvo pumping appliances with s6400.1–4, registered E570 – E573 AJO. The first, seen here, was stationed at Didcot and Chipping Norton, used as a reserve and then sent to County Kildare as 88-KE-4269 for further service. Oxfordshire has a history of formal arrangements for second users, with many of its appliances going to Malta for instance. (*HCB-Angus*)

Plate 31: Cornwall Fire Service's first Mercedes 1222 water tender ladders, registered G279 – G283 CRL, built on s6448.1–4, are pictured just after delivery. A further four similar appliances were to be ordered the following year. (*HCB-Angus*)

Plate 32: The Zambian authorities placed an order for eight appliances built, unusually, on the Leyland Comet chassis. One of the group is seen here outside the works and without its ladders. They were built on s6485.1–8 and, unfortunately, no technical details are known. Some years later, one of the group was spotted operating on a West Indian island! (*HCB-Angus*)

This later variant is a Navy version painted in all-over day-glo red – otherwise, it was to the same specification as the others. This series three Land Rover was one of a pair; s5651.1–2, registered 91 RN 48 and 49. (*HCB-Angus Archive*)

Ralf Nader's publication in the mid-1960s of *Unsafe at any Speed* highlighted the subject of vehicle safety, be it passenger car, bus or commercial vehicle. HCB-Angus for its part was equally concerned with personal safety. The cab structure of the Bedford TK that HCB-Angus was producing in numbers at the time was merely some timber with a thin fibreglass covering, a fact I was rather aware of when driving the one in my ownership, s2336, SAG 982J. HCB-Angus commissioned an in-house study of fire appliance accidents, asking all UK brigades to provide details of accidents occurring to appliances of all manufacture – not just its own. This provided a document so damning of existing design that the company decided major action should be undertaken.

Cranfield Institute of Technology and the Motor Industry Research Association (MIRA) were taken on board as technical consultants and Ogle Design as design consultants to produce a new vehicle, though HCB-Angus undertook much of the actual work themselves. The result was to be the CSV (Crew Safety Vehicle) water tender, the first vehicle designed with the safety of the crew as paramount consideration.

The press release produced at the time of the CSV's introduction at the Harrogate Fire Fighting and Equipment Exhibition in October 1976 said:

Fire fighting and emergency vehicles are pushed up to and sometimes beyond their limits to reach emergencies. In these high-risk circumstances collisions and vehicle rollovers do occur before the scene of the incident is reached. The C.S.V cab is designed to give extra -protection to the crew during this high-risk period. It meets all current requirements of the Government's joint committee on design and development and will meet also all anticipated intentional and U.K, structural regulations.

At the request of HCB-Angus, the Motor Industry Research Associations prepared a series of design requirements based on its knowledge of commercial vehicle, bus and car behaviour under crash conditions. These were supplemented by information on the extreme conditions of service met by fire fighting vehicles.

In addition HCB-Angus followed the recommendations of a number of county fire authorities. The cab design of the C.S.V. Water tender Type B was based on stringent standards evolved to cover the following design aspects relevant to real crash situations: -

1. Protection afforded to the occupants in frontal impact.
2. Energy absorption capacity of the roof structure during a rollover situation.
3. The strength of the water tank mountings.
4. Energy absorption capacity of the door structure to side intrusion.
5. Strength of door latches and hinges
6. Strength of seat fixings
7. Injury potential of interior fittings.

The company then produced a full-scale model all-metal B type Water tender to conventional build standards. The vehicle was used to establish basic ergonomic layout, general styling and prototype structure.

Structural Design
Analysis of the conventional structure showed that it required considerable modification to meet the standards evolved for the C.S.V. cab. Cranfield School of Automotive Studies had been working with HCB-Angus for some time on body structural analysis techniques. It was therefore decided to carry out both elastics and plastic deformation analyses on the cab structure using Cranfield's expertise. Cranfield performed the major part of the cab analysis on the University of Birmingham ICL 1906A computer using a finite element program capable of modelling large deflections and plastic behaviour. An elastic analysis was initially undertaken to gain an understanding of structural behaviour. Results were compared with data obtained from a load test carried out by HCB-Angus, and after modification of the preliminary model a satisfactory agreement was obtained. The elastic idealisation was retained for use at a later stage in the project, in case any further calculations were needed. Since its more complex techniques required greater computing power the plastic analysis idealisation had to be much coarser than the elastic idealisation. On the basis of the elastic calculations a reduced mathematical model was therefore devised and used for calculations in the collapse behaviour. The door strength analysis was performed solely as a hand calculation. Throughout the project emphasis was placed entirely on

strength rather than stiffness. This analysis and design method is a. departure from conventional trends and is unique in the automotive industry. An early prototype C.S.V cab and a pre-production cab were both subjected to roof crush and frontal impact tests at MIRA's Nuneaton testing ground.

Roof Crush during a roll over situation.
To simulate this condition the cab was tilted through an angle of 25 degrees and crushed on its top corner with a load in excess of twice the laden front axle weight. The roof crush sustained by the pre-production cab was less than 2" when subjected to an eight tons load, and there were no signs of impending failure.
The crushing of a tilted cab is a much more rigorous test than the widely used horizontal roof crush test which only tests the buckling strength of the cab pillars. Structural failures in roll over situations have shown how pillar bending strength capacity due to a lateral dynamic loading is vital to increase safety during rollover.

Frontal Impact
Both cabs, after being subjected to the roof crush test, were then tested for frontal impact resistance on the critical front corner of the cab. The cabs were obliquely impacted on their nearside front corner by a mass of 1000 kg
(2200 Ib) of 34 km/hr (21 m.p.h.) at a point approximately level with the top of the horizontal squab of the officer's seat just below the "H" point where the windscreen meets the corner post.
Both cabs successfully withstood the impact and maintained a good survival space for their occupants

Interior Design
Whilst designing the Crew Safety Vehicle, HCB-ANGUS made some notable improvements in the interior design of the cab of the vehicle. Ogle Design Limited of Letchworth who are experienced in vehicle interior and exterior styling were engaged to assist with the design of this completely new cab interior which combines safety, comfort and practicability
The special features incorporated into the cab included:-
1. Ergonomic design to give a 6-man crew maximum comfort and convenience
2. A completely new facia design, which forms the focal centre of the cab. Strategically placed black nylon coated steel tube grab handles are fitted.
3. All the trim is waterproof and is a rugged material to meet the needs of today's professional firemen.
4. Sound absorbent materials have been used to ensure that the cab meets JCDD noise level requirements.
5. Good cab interior lighting from a protected florescent light strip.
6. There are locations for four sets of breathing apparatus in the crew compartment which can be donned by the crew whilst in the normal sitting position, each breathing apparatus has its own conveniently placed quick release handle. Individual inertia reel lap straps are built in with the crew seating.

The cab of a Bedford TK fitted with a crew safety cage is shown undergoing a corner crush test at the MIRA testing facility. This cage was developed from the work done in the design and development of the cab for the Crew Safety Vehicle, which underwent an identical testing program. (*HCB-Angus Archive*)

The same cab, having been corner crushed, is then subjected to this corner impact test from a large chain-hung weight. With only a few modifications, the cab met with the computer-generated predictions as to safety performance. (*HCB-Angus Archive*)

7. Crew helmets are conveniently located on the low bulkhead opposite the crew seats.
8. Considerable attention has been given to purpose built pockets within the cab. Special notice boards have been provided on the cant rail section.
9. Special attention has been given to ensure that cab interior fittings meet the safety standards set by the ECE (Economic Commission for Europe) Regulation 21.
10. Excellent all round vision is available for all members of the crew, the front windscreen is laminated and all side windows are of toughened glass. An adjustable sunblind is fitted.

The use of the Bedford KG-500 chassis re-affirms the HCB-Angus policy of building their fire engines on standard, commercial chassis and not resorting to specialised chassis. Their policy has a considerable number of advantages: -
1. Readily available chassis.
2. A proven chassis, with good handling characteristics assured through the extensive development work that commercial chassis are subject to.
3. Worldwide servicing facilities.
4. Good spares back up
5. The price advantages that volume production, gives over the specialist chassis.

Note: Two special plus features are: -
1. The Bedford KG500 chassis meets the stringent Home Office braking requirements for Fire Appliances.
2. The standard engine on the KG500 is the Bedford diesel 8198 cc (500.3 cu.in.) six cylinder engine which develops 119.2 kW (159.7 b.h.p.) at 2800 rev/min.

For those customers that prefer a petrol engine HCB Angus offer the option of the Rolls Royce B61 70H/1 4887 cc (298 cu in) 6-cylinder engine which develops 131.1kW (176bhp) Installed at 4000rpm

Alongside the press release and exhibition at Harrogate, HCB-Angus engaged in a high-profile publicity campaign to raise awareness of the appliance. A 16 mm colour film was commissioned and shown to brigades around the world and massive paper publicity was undertaken under the banner of 'Arrive and Alert in the CSV'. The appliance demonstrated at Harrogate, together with another, was taken around the country to show to brigades. They were painted white to show them as something special and even gained a slot on *Blue Peter*, with Peter Perves being a fireman for the day.

The company dedicated an area of the factory to produce the CSV, utilising jigs and fixtures on a much greater scale than with the usual run of appliances. In fact, the company produced cabs to hold in stock against future orders, a process not normally undertaken. It should be noted that the rear part of the body was made to normal standards and was not crash-proofed.

In all, 121 Bedford chassis were fitted with the CSV cab, the vast majority being engineered as water tender or as water tender ladders, but there were a few special appliances; s5937, registered BCY 679V, was built for BP Chemicals as a water foam tender; s6061, registered KDC 312Y, was built as a dry powder appliance for ICI Billingham; and s6167 was the only one built as a high-top appliance, bodied out as an emergency tender for Bahrain. The UK military had three specials; these were the convoy support vehicles that used to accompany nuclear warhead convoys on their travels (colloquially known as Sunshine Convoys to the military!). They were standard water tenders but carried no ladders other than a short extension and the roofline was correspondingly built with a smooth curve front to rear. Internally, the seating was upgraded to Brostrom sprung seats for all the crew who, of course, spent many hours sat in them! They were registered 31 AG 47, 48, and 49, on s5890.1 – 3.

In an unusual arrangement, HCB-Angus supplied Fulton & Wylie Ltd of Ayrshire with twenty-nine fire engineered CSV chassis cabs for them to construct their own rear bodywork.

It was impossible for the company to produce the CSV without taking some action with the basic Bedford TK-based water tender appliance. This was immensely popular and was selling in large numbers around the world so, working with the data that the company had, the design of the appliance was modified to include a roll cage that went a long way to protect the crews. The protection did not include the door intrusion factors of the CSV but in terms of frontal collision and roll over, it was equally viable. This was, in effect, the company shooting itself in the foot in a way; the CSV was considerably more expensive than the roll-caged version of the standard vehicle with only a modicum of extra protection, albeit with more flair! The CSV had its own sales undercut in this way and was not the money-spinner the company had hoped for.

The company's energies were not just concentrated on the CSV. As mentioned earlier, the Dodge K850 series of chassis had started to be used, the first being for Perth and Kinross Fire Brigade on s2407, 8, and 9, registered RES 144J, RGS 959J and SES 268J. The Ford D series closely followed, first used for Lancashire County Fire Brigade as dual-purpose appliances on s2474 – s2484, registered LTC 390K – LTC 406K (though the last pair were re-registered STB 441J and 442J due to late delivery). There had in fact been an earlier use of Ford D chassis but this was a Simon Engineering PHP built on a Ford D1070 for Cumberland Fire Brigade, s2462, registered DRM 620K. Both the Dodge and Ford chassis saw many orders placed for them by UK brigades, making some inroads into the invincibility of the Bedford TK. For instance, Greater Manchester Fire Brigade placed an order for no less than forty Ford D1617 appliances at one time, s5611.1–20 and s5612.1–20. This was not reflected abroad, where the 4x2 and 4x4 Bedfords reigned almost supreme. An interesting derivation of the standard Bedford TK water tender was that developed for the overseas market. The TK wheelbase was not shortened but was fitted with a standard-style water tender body and a 1,000-gallon water tank rather than the UK standard 400-gallon tank. Indeed, for some orders the tank was capable of holding 1,800 gallons of water. These appliances had full crew cabs and were fully equipped and not, therefore, to be confused with water carriers, which had merely an elliptical tank and PTO-driven pump. Nigeria (where many were to go) had the first of these, on s5081.1 and 2. The cab front differed from normal production in as much as the cab was standard Bedford to the rear of the doors but the roofline was moulded to a peak rather than the smooth curve normally provided.

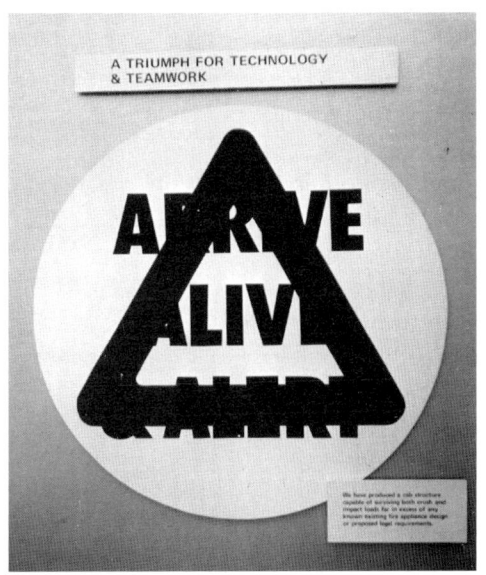

Right: 'Arrive Alive and Alert' was the motto coined to go with the announcement of the new Crew Safety Vehicle. As it says in the statement, the cab strength far outstripped any current or potential legislative requirements. (*HCB-Angus Archive*)

Below: A CSV cab structure fresh from the construction jigs. Note that all four doors are part of the structure and, like the rest of the cab, are constructed from high-grade rectangular section steel. (*HCB-Angus Archive*)

An artist's illustration demonstrating the integration of the safety cab within the whole vehicle. The rear body, behind the crew section, was not constructed to the same standards. (*HCB-Angus Archive*)

A dedicated part of the factory was set up just for building the CSV. The jigs were permanent fixtures and all the various parts could be brought together with the minimum of disturbance and disruption. (*HCB-Angus Archive*)

One of the demonstrators waits patiently in the yard before going for exhibition at the Chief Fire Officers' Conference. The paintwork, white with a red stripe, was chosen just to stand out – later, the Isle of Wight Fire Brigade took the colour scheme on board for the CSVs that it ordered. (*HCB-Angus Archive*)

Three special CSVs were constructed for the MoD, s5890.1–3. They were basic water tenders but without the ladder assemblies and were fitted with up-rated seating. They were convoy support units for the nuclear warhead convoys and were registered 31AG 47 – 49. (*HCB-Angus Archive*)

s5937, registered BCY 679Y, was the only foam tender constructed on the CSV appliance base. It was built for the Baglan Bay Refinery on an order from BP. (*HCB-Angus Archive*)

Hampshire Fire and Rescue Service ordered a number of CSV appliances over a period of years. Here is OOW 57S, one of a group of four, s5740.1–4, registered OOW 55S – 58S, fresh from the paint shop and at that time devoid of all stripes and lettering. All Hampshire's appliances acquired wind deflectors low down on the front corners in an attempt to keep the side windows clear of rain. (*HCB-Angus Archive*)

A pair of left-hand drive CSVs awaiting delivery to Bahrain. This country ordered three groups of these appliances as water tenders and one special, constructed as an emergency tender. This had a Hi Top but so as not to compromise the cab structure, the high roof was a false one built over the original. (*HCB-Angus Archive*)

One design feature that caused some headaches for the company was the fact that the Dodge K and Ford D series, like the AECs before them, had a tilt cab. This meant that the re-design work to create a crew cab from the scuttle backwards was not possible on these chassis. The crew space was provided fixed to the chassis and communication with the front cab was by way of a hatch, also not good for the crew's forward visibility. On the other hand, the Bedfords had a good crew cab, with a full-width half-bulkhead, but had very difficult access for engine and gearbox maintenance. There are stories of brigades cutting holes in the roof of the cab to enable engines to be craned out (the approved method was to take it out from underneath by first removing the front axle or by way of the driver's door, but it was a tricky job). Tilt cabs would become a thorny subject later in the development of the company's appliances.

At the smaller end of the scale, the introduction of the Bedford CF van by Vauxhall Motors in 1970 required HCB-Angus to produce an appliance based on it; given the close link with Vauxhall Motors, the company could hardly refuse! The first of these s2355 (unregistered) went to Vauxhall Motors themselves as a works appliance, followed by a few other single-vehicle orders, mostly to industrial brigades. In 1973 the Egyptian government placed on order for no less than fifty appliances, s5328.1–50. From then on, the Transit and the CF were in stiff competition in the light fire appliances market.

Early in the 1970s the last AEC chassis passed through the works; a pumping appliance for Dublin City Fire Brigade, s5144, registered 5220 ZC. The AEC, with its stylish ergonomic cab, made a handsome looking appliance. Land Rover continued to be used for worldwide deliveries of light 4x4 appliances of all descriptions, never in

As part of the major publicity effort with the CSV, the company managed to persuade *Blue Peter*, the children's TV program, to do a piece on the appliance. Here Peter Purves, who presented the item, is dismounting the officer's seat. (*HCB-Angus Archive*)

huge numbers for any one order (with the exception of the MoD) but continuously to every conceivable type of user.

Chassis from the American Dodge W300 and W400 series (the Power Wagon) were taken on and saw some success. These were bonnetted pickups typical of the American market and were foreseen as the basis for a fast road-going vehicle, with some off road capability, for rescue and airfield use. Powered by a typically large V8 petrol engine, they were indeed fast but consumed large quantities of fuel. There is a story that one brigade, which used them as motorway rescue tenders, was unable to send them to the far end of their territory as they could not carry enough fuel to get them back to base. The carrying of Jerry cans of fuel became normal practice. The first Power Wagon was s5518, ordered by the government of Dubai for use at Dubai International Airport, after which the model met some success around the world. The UK was not too keen on the vehicle, although Teesside Airport took one, s5592, registered RGP472P, as did Tresco Airport on the Isles of Scilly, s5813, registered JHO 551S. It was not until the twin rear-wheeled version appeared that some success was seen, Fife Fire Brigade taking up the HCB-Angus demonstrator, originally s5860 and re numbered s5929, registered PCG 972T, as a road rescue unit.

There was an odd development in the co-operation with Unipower (Universal Power Drives Ltd of Middlesex) in the use of its Invader chassis for the basis of a crash tender.

Unipower was a small company anxious to get into the commercial and military vehicle market, to which end they produced various vehicles on a 4x4 chassis. HCB-Angus took up a chassis in 1972, s5241, and developed the vehicle to crash tender specification. For this vehicle, a new all-fibreglass cab front was developed. But success was not to be. During the decade only two orders for single vehicles were received and the Malaysian government put some faith in Unipower by placing two orders for nine and eight vehicles respectively, s5411.1–9 and s5421.1–8. Unipower later took up the reins where Leyland left off with the Scammell crash tenders (again descended from Thornycroft) and continued to produce crash tenders for the aviation scene. Latterly, the company was purchased by Alvis Ltd and effectively ceased to exist in 1994 when Alvis put the company up for sale.

It was suggested, and taken up, that this new scuttle might be used to update the Bedford TK front and several vehicles were produced for the UK market. Inevitably, they were to cost more than the existing model and sales were not good. All in all, only about twenty vehicles were to receive this cab treatment.

The Ministry of Defence (RAF) placed an order in March 1971 for twenty-seven small domestic appliances, s5038.1–27, based on the small Bedford KB chassis, with six stud wheels. Equipped with a 100-gallon tank (later orders had a 150-gallon tank), Godiva pump and a single hose reel. These little appliances were somewhat dwarfed by the 35-foot aluminium ladder they carried, which protruded rather a long way out front. This order was followed by two orders for one and two of these appliances but was followed up a decade later by another order for a significant number, s6308.1–13.

An order was placed for a pair of unusual looking triple-agent vehicles, s5167.1 and 2, for the Chilean oil industry. Based on Ford D series three-axle trucks, they carried 1,300 gallons of water in an elliptical tank and 200 gallons of foam, delivered by way of a roof monitor, six hand lines and a hose reel. Added to this were 300 lbs of carbon dioxide in fixed cylinders and a 45-foot ladder mounted atop the tank. These were the replacement vehicles for the Leyland Comet appliances mentioned earlier.

Late in the 1960s, Warwickshire Fire Brigade found themselves in urgent need of a bulk foam carrier and HCB-Angus obliged by converting a Bedford S petrol tanker in to a foam carrier, s2078, registered VYT 148. Five years later, its replacement was a purpose built vehicle, this time a Bedford TK-based appliance, s5310, registered PNX 999M.

Mention should be made of the Thornycroft Nubians that went through the works in a steady stream as crash tenders, with no order being the same as any other. Body serials 5176.1–3 were a trio of Thornycroft Nubian Mk 1 6x6 vehicles for Dubai. With minimal rear bodywork, they carried 1,450 gallons of water and 200 of foam compound delivered via side-mounted hand lines and a roof monitor. From time to time there were orders for a suite of vehicles. Entebbe Airport, Uganda, ordered a Nubian crash tender, s5237, and a Bedford M rescue unit, s5238, at the same time, presumably to upgrade existing vehicles at one stroke.

Remarked on earlier was a breakdown lorry constructed for Durham Fire Brigade, one of only three constructed by the company. The third of the trio was s5217, again on

The Unipower Invader chassis provided the basis for this airfield crash tender, HCB-Angus developing a fibreglass scuttle for it (this was also seen on some Bedford appliances). Not a very popular choice, the only orders came from Qatar, who had the demonstrator (s5241, becoming s5497) and s5280, and Malaysia, who had two batches, s5411.1–9 and 5742.1–9. (*HCB-Angus Archive*)

s5038.1–27, one of which is shown here on its second life, were twenty-seven small appliances for the MoD on the Bedford TKB chassis. Registered 23 AJ 79 – 99 and 24 AJ 00 – 05, they were somehow designed with the peaked cab roof more usually reserved for the big T10 water tenders that went abroad. (*Photographer unknown*)

This rather ungainly-looking appliance, s5167, a Ford DT 1700, is one of a pair of refinery machines for the Chilean oil industry. As in the earlier example, it tends to the American practice of hanging kit on the outside rather than using lockers. (*HCB-Angus Archive*)

When Warwickshire Fire Brigade needed a foam carrier in a hurry, HCB-Angus converted a petrol tanker for duty. This Bedford S was s2078, registered VYT 148. (*HCB-Angus Archive*)

The venerable S type was eventually replaced some six years later by s5210, a Bedford TK registered PNX 999M. Longwell Green, Bristol, in fact built this vehicle, in common with many fire engines that needed large-capacity elliptical tanks, as a sub-contract. (*HCB-Angus Archive*)

a Bedford 4x4, and this time to go abroad to Iraq. In common with other Bedfords going abroad, this had a full Bedford cab fitted with the HCB-Angus peaked cab front.

In among the large numbers of Bedford TK, Dodge K and Ford D chassis for the domestic market that flowed through the works (not counting the steady stream of Land Rovers) were a number of strangers. One such was s5210, a Leyland Mastiff that was constructed as an emergency tender for Nottingham City Fire Brigade. This was registered EAU 999L. Being an ET, there was no need for a drive line power take off, the extra electrical energy for the various lighting and rescue equipment being provided by a generator belt-driven direct from the engine. Another Leyland product produced was for Iraq (s5266.1 and 2). These were badged as Albion but were cabbed with the standard LAD cab of the day. This pair was really strange as they were, unusually, converted to four-wheel drive but as they were for use in the desert, this would have been very useful.

The British Petroleum operation in Norway had a need for a pair of refinery foam tenders and ordered them from HCB-Angus on s5399.1 and 2 early in 1973. They were based on the Dodge KT900 chassis, the heaviest, fitted with a second rear axle. They carried 600 gallons of foam compound in a stainless steel tank and were equipped with a Godiva pump for delivery of foam once supported with hydrant water feed. They were also equipped with Albany pumps for the re-filling of the main tank from bulk storage. The hand-line deliveries were fitted at the rear but, unusually for a refinery foam tender, they carried no roof-mounted monitor.

A steady stream of Nubian crash tenders went through the works, with no two orders being the same. This one, rather bereft of bodywork, was one of three for Dubai built against s5176.1–3. Tough machines, they carried 1,450 gallons of water, 200 gallons of foam and had a mid-mounted pump feeding the monitor and hand lines. Notice the HCB-Angus numbered build plate on the rear nearside, a feature of all but a very few machines.

One pair of Land Rovers ordered by the Indonesian government on s5446.1 and 2 had a varied life. They were strange in design, being light pumps with a standard crew carrying capability. To this end they were long wheelbase hard tops and the rear door had to be omitted as the pump protruded beyond the rear of the vehicle by some 250 mm. A rather odd locker had to be constructed to cover this with a roller shutter. When the time came, the customer had had a change of heart and the order was not shipped. Being non-standard appliances, the company had difficulty in finding a customer for them and they hung around the works for nearly two years before Cornwall Fire Brigade purchased them. They were refurbished and became s5662.1 and 2, registered MCV 569 and 570V. One of the pair eventually went on to serve at Tresco in the Isles of Scilly.

An interesting trio of vehicles came into the works for a complete re-fit. These were the three coach-built Bedford RLs, s5321.1–3, registered 12 AJ 05, 06 and 07, that had been built some years earlier by Marshall of Cambridge as support vehicles for the helicopters of the Queen's Flight. Wherever a Royal personage was to land or take off in a helicopter, one of these appliances was present. They were equipped to a high level with re-fuelling, communications and fire-fighting equipment. However, they had been equipped with BCF (bromochlorodiflouromethane) fire-fighting equipment in the first instance before it was recognised that this material presented a health risk in its own right. These three vehicles came in to be re-fitted with carbon dioxide and foam-

The Leyland Mastiff was an odd choice for a fire engine chassis. This one, s5210, registered EAU 999L, was built up as an emergency tender for Nottingham City Fire Brigade. (*HCB-Angus Archive*)

A rather strange-looking LAD cabbed 4x4 emergency tender built for Iran. Three were built on s5266.1–3 and delivered to that country's military. (*HCB-Angus Archive*)

A pair of refinery tenders was built for the BP Norwegian operation on the Dodge KT900 chassis on s5399.1-2. They were a little odd in as much as no roof monitor was fitted, all operations being by hand line. They carried 600 gallons of foam compound, relying on the mains hydrants for their water supply. (*HCB-Angus Archive*)

making equipment and were given a general upgrading all round and went on to serve the Queen's Flight for another 12 years.

The next major chassis adaptation came with the Commer G11 series, the Commando. The first of these, with chrome-plated bumpers, etc. as it was an exhibition vehicle, was s5491, registered LRD 721P, for the United Kingdom Atomic Energy Authority site at Harwell. It was a standard water tender ladder in format but as a new chassis, it required the company to make a number of modifications to the placement of components before starting work on the fire engineering. These included the provision of yet another version of the company's sandwich-style power take off. Devon Fire Brigade was the first local fire authority to take up this chassis, ordering nine water tenders on s5507.1-9, registered LTT 196P – 205P. Oddly, these appliances were specified with the top-hinged 'slam'-style locker covers, by this time a rare feature.

In 1978 the Nigerian government ordered a trio of large emergency tenders on the Bedford M chassis, s5720.1-3, fitted with the Bedford petrol engine (many of the non UK deliveries were still petrol powered). Unusually for an emergency tender, they were fitted with a typical fire appliance cab with seating for six persons as well as a full height body. The vehicle engine drove a 7 kVA generator running at 110 volts by way of the standard power take-off. As was often the case with vehicles going abroad, the company fully kitted the appliance with all its equipment. The manifest ran to over three pages of closely typed script with items ranging from a screwdriver and a pair of pliers right through to a large, lorry-sized trolley jack and electrically driven rescue equipment. All this had to be racked up in the vehicle before delivery.

An experiment tried by the company was the production of a 'Lo Cost' water tender where the chassis production cab was retained in its entirety for the driver and officer. The rear body was a box construction in which the crew had a compartment at the front end – with no communication with the cab. Cheap they were, popular they were not! The design was first tried in the 1960s on the Ford D chassis and ordered only by Gloucestershire Fire Service and was re-tried now with the Bedford TK chassis. The Bedford prototype, s5764, eventually ended up in Zambia. The third and last order, sometime later, was from the MoD for nine appliances on the Bedford TL chassis, s6409.1–9, registered in the 48 KG ?? series.

The late 1970s were quite difficult times, orders having dropped off and the company finding itself having to build appliances without having buyers for them: 'product build' or else lay off workers at the factory. This was an expensive business as chassis had to be paid for before work could be undertaken in the build of vehicles. The difficulties of working with some foreign customers did not help. One client from the near Middle East spent some years negotiating a specification and price for a vehicle only to pull out for political reasons when the vehicle was just about complete. This left HCB-Angus with a well-nigh unique vehicle on its hands. This was eventually sold to another customer at a knockdown price to get rid of it, only to have the original client come back some months later wanting the vehicle. He was somewhat upset that the second build was more expensive than he had agreed to in the first place. In all, nearly six years went by from the time of the original enquiry to delivery of the vehicle!

The last major development of the decade was the construction of a prototype airfield crash tender on the Scammell Nubian Major Mk 2 chassis. This chassis was the first use by HCB-Angus of the new generation Nubians, fitted with a Cummins engine mounted at the rear, driving all six wheels by way of an Allison auto gearbox. The vehicle was built with a 2,000-gallon water tank, a 200-gallon foam tank, single cab-top mounted monitor, a pair of under-front bumper mounted foam monitors and no less than four hand lines. The vehicle did not become a demonstrator, as did the majority of prototype vehicles; in fact, it was sold before completion and became s5929, going to Air Rianta, where it served at Cork Airport for over twenty years.

The end of the decade saw a 'slight' error with a fortunate (for the company) ending. The company built a Dodge Power Wagon appliance to go to Cyprus for duty at Larnaca Airport. It joined ship at Southampton painted red but it was realised, once it was on the high seas, that it should have been yellow. The company made arrangements for it to be re painted immediately it landed - at no small expense. However, while crossing the Bay of Biscay in a storm, the bulldozer that the Dodge shared hold space with broke loose and crashed around. The Dodge suffered considerably (axles bent, panels destroyed etc) and was written off the moment it was landed on the dock in Limassol. The insurance company paid for another, which went out to Cyprus painted yellow. The original one was s6038 and its replacement was s6132.

The Commer Commando (G series) offered HCB-Angus a new, more modern chassis to work with. Here we see the prototype, carrying rather more chrome than would normally be the case; this was built on s5491. After doing the rounds on trade plates, it was eventually registered as LRX721P and entered service with UKAEA Harwell. (*HCB-Angus Archive*)

Devon Fire Brigade was the first to take up the Commando as a domestic water tender. LTP 198P was one of nine in the order, s5507.1–9, registered LTT 196P – 205P. Note the top-hung locker doors, unusual at this point in time and adopted, apparently, for no other reason than that the brigade had some earlier appliances so fitted. (*HCB-Angus Archive*)

Nigeria had its quota of strange machines; here is a very large emergency tender on a 4x4 Bedford M. There were three on s5720.1–3. The company also fitted out these appliances, to the last screwdriver! (*HCB-Angus Archive*)

HCB-Angus had several attempts at Lo Cost vehicles (manufacturer's cab plus separate body, including a crew space) but they were not hugely successful. The first examples were purchased by Gloucestershire Fire Brigade, s1429–1431, registered KDF 454E and 455E and LAD 228E. (*HCB-Angus Archive*)

The second attempt, based on the TK cab, saw less success, the one and only going to Zambia; however, the third, with the Bedford TL cab, produced one order from the MoD for the RAF for nine appliances. Built on s6409.1–9, they were variously registered in the 48 KG ?? series. (*HCB-Angus Archive*)

The introduction of the Nubian Major Mk 2 required a huge amount of work from the company, as the chassis was a mile away in design from the previous version. However, the prototype, s5929, registered 960 DZB, went to Air Rianta and saw its whole service life at Cork International Airport. When the author was speaking to the airport about its life, he was told, 'Oh, she was a fine machine, worked well for over twenty years and made a fine pile of scrap when we cut her up!' Praise indeed! (*HCB-Angus Archive*)

A view of the classic Bedford TK water tender ladder. Equipped with a 400 gallon tank, 500 gallon per minute pump and a 45-foot ladder as basic kit, they were manufactured in their hundreds and sent around the world. (*HCB-Angus Archive*)

Built for the Brecon and Radnor Joint Fire Brigade, this heavy-duty Bedford TK has had its Bedford diesel engine removed and replaced with a Perkins V8 unit, had been to Simon Engineering to have 70-foot booms fitted and then been bodied by the company prior to delivery to the brigade. Built with body s5017, it was registered FFO 606K. (*HCB-Angus Archive*)

7
The 1980s

The 1980s were to be a troubled time for the company. As mentioned in the history section, there was a financial crisis and problems with labour, causing a considerable reduction in staff and a cutback in production. Decisions had to be made about what type of vehicles to seek contracts for and what markets to pursue. The company recovered part way through the decade and the variety of vehicles produced returned to its previous levels, although staffing levels and the number of vehicles produced did not.

The company returned to the fray in seeking orders from London Fire Brigade. Apart from the trio of ERFs, it had done little for this brigade – just an experimental first strike appliance based on the Bedford CF van, s5134, registered JLT 1K, re registered MGY 1L. However, in 1982 the company tendered for thirty-six pumping appliances based on the Dodge G13 chassis. The development appliance was on s6120, registered KUV 659X, and the bulk of the order was on s6131.1–35, registered KUV 660X – 695X. While the vehicles in themselves were nothing out of the ordinary, the process of development and eventual delivery was not a good one for the company and further orders were not pursued.

The London Salvage Corps (in no way connected with the London Fire Brigade, other than in sharing radio facilities) took delivery of two vehicles from HCB-Angus. The Salvage Corps, disbanded in 1984, worked alongside the fire brigade, not to extinguish fire but to prevent or reduce incidental damage to property by water, smoke, falling debris and exposure to the weather. Its tenders shared many similarities with emergency tenders and so fell within the company's sphere of work. The two appliances were s5339, registered ULM 743M, on a Dodge K850 and s6254, registered ALY 911Y, on a Dodge G13. The former had a complete crew cab but the rear was a box body with access to all the equipment from inside, whereas the latter could easily be mistaken for a water tender as this was basically how it was constructed – just without the water tank and pump.

The TACR appliances that HCB-Angus first pioneered so many years before were now well into their service lives. Indeed, many had already been cast off service and had been replaced by the MoD with a Range Rover-based appliance known as the TACR2. Carmichael & Sons (Worcester) Ltd, the company's fiercest competitor,

The company had another attempt at the London Fire Brigade market with these Dodge G1313 appliances. The first, s6120, registered KUV 659X, the development vehicle, was followed by the main order of 6131.1–35, registered KUV 660X – 694X. The company did not find the experience to be a good one and did not return to this market. (*HCB-Angus Archive*)

The London Salvage Corps ran a number of very specialist vehicles, as their purpose was not to fight fires but to minimise damage and save property. They had two vehicles from HCB-Angus, the first being a Dodge K850-based vehicle, s5929, registered ULF 743M. (*HCB-Angus Archive*)

The second, s6154, registered ALY 911Y, was on a Commer G1313 chassis. As can be seen from this locker shot, they carried a great array of special equipment for damage limitation purposes. (*HCB-Angus Archive*)

had developed this vehicle and produced a number together with Gloster Saro Ltd. HCB-Angus tendered for and received a contract for eighteen of these appliances to be produced in 1982. The development appliance (s6159, eventually registered 94 AM 37) was ordered in January 1982 and was rapidly followed by the bulk order on s6163.1–17, registered 31 AG 52 – 61 and 51 AG 46 – 52. The work on the first appliance ran some weeks ahead of the main bulk of vehicles and this was the one closely inspected by the MoD. Any errors, alterations or corrections identified were rectified and applied to the remainder. HCB-Angus did not undertake the third axle conversion; this was completed by Carmichael Ltd. These TACR2s were painted in NATO infrared-reflective paint, a singularly unbecoming green colour!

It is understood (though the records are missing and the evidence is meagre) that the company built fifteen further similar appliances for Abu Dhabi under s6319.1–9 and s6320.1–6. These may have been only 4x4 vehicles based on the TACR2 concept and they were described as rescue tenders.

Staying with the Rover Company for a while, Land Rovers had been the basis of a range of appliances that were dispatched all over the world which, while varied in scope, had retained the hinged locker layout during the whole production period; there was just not the room for roller shutters of any size. With Land Rover development vehicle s5938, the company tried something new: a large, one-piece, offset, top-hinged 'cupboard'-style locker along the length of both sides. This became known affectionately as the 'fish fryer' style of locker. The prototype, returned to works after a period on loan to the Isle of Wight Fire Brigade, was refurbished and converted to left-

The TACR1s now being 20 years old, the MoD sought a replacement and the Range Rover 6x6 conversion by Carmichael formed such a basis. Built also by Carmichael and by Gloster Saro, the TACR2 was an imposing vehicle. Here is shown one of the main HCB-Angus order for seventeen on s6163.1–17, registered 31 AG 53 – 61 and 51 AG 46 – 52. (*HCB-Angus Archive*)

A three-quarter rear view showing the hand line branch and its hose flaked into the carrier.

The body building area. The nearer appliance is having its cab framing built up and as yet no fire engineering has been installed. The rear of the pair, demonstrating the degree of articulation of the rear pair of axles, is not in fact an HCB-Angus product – it was a Gloster Saro vehicle loaned by the RAF for evaluation purposes. (*HCB-Angus Archive*)

hand drive to join s5985.1–15 for service with the Iranian Oil Company. Land Rover continued to form the basis of appliances throughout the decade and beyond.

In the same year (1983) the company received its second and final order for a Scammell Nubian Mk 2 6x6 crash tender, s6278, registered MP481, this time to go to Barbados. Built to the same technical specification as the one that went to Cork Airport but with a somewhat different body style, it was in fact not built by HCB-Angus but was sub-contracted to Carmichael Ltd, although it was badged as HCB-Angus. Conditions at the company at the time were such that it was just not able to tackle such a large and complex job.

The 1980s also saw the last incarnation of the ubiquitous Bedford TK. This time, the whole cab was designed from scratch, not all-metal as in the CSV but with a stylish all-fibreglass front end and tubular steel framed cab. Described by the company as the HSC (High Strength Cab), it was well received and considerable numbers were built. There was one problem, however, with its construction. The company had always undertaken its own fibreglass work in house but with increasing restrictions on working practices by the Health and Safety lobby and, in this case, formal complaints from neighbours about the styrene fumes coming from the moulding shop, fabrication was contracted out to Moore Plastics in Kent. The demonstrator, s5975, was developed during the late 1970s and was announced in 1980. The first order placed for this version of the TK was from Cambridge Fire and Rescue Service in 1982 on s5995.1–2, registered BVA 15 and 16V. The demonstrator was eventually refurbished as s6038, registered BTP 483W, and joined Hampshire Fire Brigade.

Maybe not the way to treat your new stock; some chassis cabs wait in the snow for their turn to enter the body shop. (*HCB-Angus Archive*)

After many years of production, some thought was given to new ways of bodying Land Rover appliances and this was the result. Nicknamed the 'fish fryer' lockers, they formed spacious bins into which kit could be placed. The lids were held open with gas struts. This example, s6220, was on its way to Indonesia. (*HCB-Angus Archive*)

The introduction of the High Strength Cab in 1980 was a further step forward. Whereas the CSV had a fixed cab, this version of the TK could be had with either a fixed cab or with the full-length tilting crew cab. Unlike the CSV, which had an all-metal cab, the HSC had a substantial GRP moulding for the scuttle assembly fronting a steel framed cab. It is not recorded where this publicity photography water tender ladder ended up. (*HCB-Angus Archive*)

This engine, plus its twin, was for Tipperary County Council Brigade and is typical of the model. They were built on s6413.1–2 and registered 998 and 999 BFI. (*HCB-Angus Archive*)

It might be worth carrying the Bedford story through to its conclusion at this point. The Bedford TK and its family had been running more or less unchanged for more than twenty years: it was decidedly out of date with its fixed cab and Bedford needed to do something about it. Thus came the TL chassis in 1981/82. While being very much based on the TK (even to having the engine access flaps on its flanks), it had a tilt cab, which brought it somewhat up to date. This in turn caused HCB-Angus a problem. Modelling of the crew cab relied on a non-tilt cab, so for their coach-built crew-cabbed version the new tilt cab became a screwed down cab! The major revision to the front was the repositioning of the headlamps to the front bumper and a change to the grille. The HSC version, of course, had an HCB-Angus designed cab fitted instead of the Bedford original and, at about this time, it was offered as a complete tilt crew cab. The development work for this had been carried out on a Dodge chassis. The tilting HSC cabs could easily be identified by the fact that the headlights, as with all TL versions, were bumper bar-mounted. The CSV was always supplied as a fixed cab as all its original design work had depended on this. Of course, the standard Bedford cab was retained for those vehicles so specified.

However, things were not to go well for Bedford and sales in the commercial world fell as its technology came to be seen as far behind the newcomers from continental Europe and the Far East; but it still came as a bit of a shock when General Motors announced that Bedford truck production was to cease. This announcement, in 1986, was made with little or no warning and caused HCB-Angus something of a problem to say the least - their principal chassis supplier shutting shop. Bedford's Dunstable plant (where trucks were built) was sold the following year to Mr David Brown, owner of AWD Ltd. The name Bedford continued on, but only on military chassis, with commercial vehicles carrying the AWD name.

This was not a happy situation for HCB-Angus; confidence in the company was not good, and the UK military moved away from AWD as its truck supplier. It came as little surprise when AWD collapsed in 1992, owing tens of millions of pounds. Marshall of Cambridge stepped in and bought the moribund company, ran down and disposed of the Dunstable plant and moved production to Cambridge, where the two and four-wheel drive versions continued at a very low level. UK fire brigades lost interest in the Bedford/AWD chassis as a basis for fire appliances as soon as the original closure was announced, so production of the new TL-chassied appliances was very limited for the home market but continued on for export markets. Base vehicles were acquired from Marshall as well as from dealer stocks from around the country.

The last CSV was ordered in 1983 for County Kildare Fire Brigade on s6283, registered 2440 ZW, after a production run of less than 125 appliances. The last HSC version, after a run of nearly 130 vehicles, comprised an order from Lincolnshire Fire Brigade for four appliances on s6365.1–4, registered D799 – 801 XTL and D906 AVL. As mentioned earlier, both CSV and HSC vehicles were offered for sale at the same time as the baseline TK machine, which continued longer than they did and at a much cheaper price – which must had something to do with the sales figures.

It was at much the same time as this was going on that the technical staff at the company were addressing a matter that had long given the company food for thought

– that of tilt cabs and crew accommodation. As mentioned when talking about the Ford D and Dodge K series of appliances, it had been of concern to the company that the crew were 'remote' from the front cab. To this end, the company pioneered the construction of a complete cab that could be tilted forward like the standard commercial cab. This made for a particularly heavy construction, as the entire cab would not be multi-point fixed to the chassis but front hinged and on catches at the rear. As the normal counterbalance springing would not be up to the task of raising such a cab, a hydraulic ram and prop system had to be devised. This did not make for a quick lift, as several minutes of hand pumping was required. The prototype was built on s6304 and toured the country, later being refurbished as s6363 and registered D527 MHB for South Glamorgan Fire Service. The design, while successful, was not hugely popular because it was expensive. Incidentally, this appliance suffered severe frontal damage in an RTC while with South Glamorgan and was rebuilt - but without the combined crew cab.

Malaysia had a need at this time to re-equip its fire service with some new vehicles, so the government approached the HCB-Angus for some midi water tenders. These were small appliances, based on standard water tender practice but scaled down. This group was based on the small Bedford TL 860 chassis and carried just 100 gallons of water but had a main pump and carried a 30-foot aluminium ladder. The order was for twenty-two of these vehicles, s6303.1–22, and the delivery schedule was quite tight. HCB-Angus were very busy at this time with their recovery program, so much so that assistance had to be sought and the order was completed by the company doing all the fire engineering on all the chassis while some (not all) were then taken to Carmichael in Worcester to be bodied. This presented a slight logistical problem, as all the appliances had to be totally identical and inspections were thorough, to say the least. The order was delivered to the docks on time!

There were a number of water carriers built for Abu Dhabi of the United Arab Emirates, which, while I suspect were not for fire fighting duties, were built along fire engine lines. Built on the Bedford KM chassis in 6x6 form, they carried a 3,000-gallon elliptical tank of stainless steel and a main engine-driven Godiva pump at the rear. There were thirty of these; s6291 was the development vehicle, while the bulk of the order was on s6292.1–29. The purchasing officer from the country, despite having seen the original specification and drawings, refused to accept the first vehicle produced as it did not look like a fire appliance (it did, indeed, only have the two-man cab from Bedford and a large elliptical tank and a rear-mounted pump). In order to progress the work and to get the vehicles accepted, the company had to construct half height lockers along both sides of the appliances. No profit in this job then!

Just sometimes, the company tendered for and received an order for a whole fire brigade. Well, if it's a small island then this can be the case. In 1981 a report was submitted to the government of the British Virgin Islands on the feasibility of creating an independent fire service for the islands and as a result the brigade was created and new equipment ordered. This came to HCB-Angus as an order for vehicles and loose equipment:

s6350: Bedford TL water tender, registered GVO 201
s6351.1 to 2: Land Rover light pumps, registered GVO 204 and 205

Dodge G1313 demonstration vehicle s6303 demonstrates the size of the tilting cab. This went on, after refurbishment, to be s6363, registered D527 MHB, for South Glamorgan. (*HCB-Angus Archive*)

This water tender for Trinidad and Tobago was one of the few Shelvoke and Drewery WX83 chassis to go through the Totton works; it was one of a pair, built on s6231.1–2. They were built with full tilting cabs, as can be seen. (*HCB-Angus Archive*)

The only Leyland Sherpa to pass through HCB-Angus hands was this little dry powder unit, s6222, built for Mobil Oil for their operation on Barbados. (*HCB-Angus Archive*)

The TLB-cabbed baby Bedford formed the basis for a very large order for midi water tenders for Malaysia, and a pretty little machine it made. Twenty-two were ordered on s6303.1–22. (*HCB-Angus Archive*)

A number of the Bedford TLB midi water tenders for Malaysia are lined up outside the factory, awaiting delivery to Southampton docks. (*HCB-Angus Archive*)

Such were the production pressures on HCB-Angus at the time that the company entered into an arrangement with Carmichael that they should body some of these appliances. Here two with the fire engineering complete are seen being loaded up for the trip to Worcester. (*HCB-Angus Archive*)

Thirty of these 2,500-gallon water carriers for Abu Dhabi were ordered on s6291, the development vehicle, and s6292.1–29. They were built to specification but delivery was not accepted by the Arab customer 'as they did not look like fire engines', so a simple box frame body had to be built over the tank assembly. (*HCB-Angus Archive*)

The very last Bedford-chassied vehicle built by HCB-Angus. The TLM cab is more pleasing to the eye than the TKM and though this was sourced from Marshall of Cambridge, it is still a Bedford! Built for the Nigerian National Petroleum Company, this pair on s6533.1–2 was quite handsome! (*HCB-Angus Archive*)

s6352.1 to 2: Bedford CF water carriers, registered GVO 208 and 210
s6353: A two-wheeled trailer with a 60-gallon foam compound tank.
s6354 and 5: Covering the supply of loose equipment

The Bedford CF water carriers were interesting vehicles as they were flatbed trucks with side and rear up-stands containing a pillow tank (a tank in the form of a flexible, tough, waterproof membrane) capable of carrying 200 gallons of water. The necessary water inlet and outlet pipe work was hard plumbed in.

The MoD continued to source appliances from the company, the first order of the decade being for thirteen midi appliances on the Bedford TL, these being small domestic appliances carrying just 150 gallons of water. They were built on s6308.1–13, being registered in two blocks, 44 KB 84–8s and 67 KC 70–80. The 'Lo Cost' concept re-appeared with an order for nine water tenders based on the Bedford TL chassis for the Royal Air Force. As with the much earlier version of this concept, the standard Bedford cab was retained and the crew travelled in a compartment in the box structure of the

This page and following: Occasionally, a whole fire service was ordered! This Bedford TL water tender, on s6350, was ordered for the British Virgin Isles Fire and Rescue Service, together with a pair of Land Rover light fire engines on 6351.1–2 and a pair of water carriers on Bedford CF flats on 6352.1–2. These last were interesting as they made use of a 200-gallon pillow tank that sat within the side and end boards of the flat. Also ordered at the same time were a pair of foam carrying trailers on 6353.1–2 and a crate of equipment. (*HCB-Angus Archive*)

rear body. These appliances had standard water tender capabilities and were built on s6409.1–9, registered 48 KG 70, 71 and 90–96. They were to be the last the last of a long line of Bedford appliances ordered by the MoD.

During the 1980s a number of Dennis chassis appeared at HCB-Angus works to be bodied. Hardly surprising, as in 1985 Dennis discontinued fire engine bodybuilding and was thus no longer a rival. Until this time, the only Dennis chassis to go through the works was an F118 Snorkel appliance for Peking but during the 1980s some forty DS and RS chassis were bodied by the company, mostly as water tender ladders. The first significant order was from Cambridge Fire and Rescue Service for four water tenders on the RS135 chassis, s6332.1–4, registered D746 to D749 KVA. Shortly after, Hampshire Fire Brigade placed an order for four on the DS153, s6372.1–4, registered E750 to E753 HRV. There was an interesting quartet (though they did span over into the 1990s) of emergency tenders ordered by North Yorkshire Fire Brigade on Dennis DS135s. Originally ordered as a pair, s6380.1–2, registered E788 and E789 LAJ, they must have impressed as two further appliances were ordered, s6435, registered G713 DAJ, and s6461, registered G713 DAJ. Though only fitted with a two-man cab, the bodying and fitting out of these vehicles was quite complex and required Dennis Specialist Vehicles to do some work on the chassis before delivery to HCB-Angus. They were very compact - the photographs show just how short they were.

HCB-Angus built many special appliances, that is, appliances that are not pumps. It is not possible to mention them all, but a pair of interesting vehicles for the UK oil refineries is worth mentioning. Built on three-axle Ford Cargo 2424 chassis, this pair of appliances, s6410, registered F222 WPR, and s6434, registered G313 DFX, was destined for the Lindsey Oil Refinery as foam tenders. They carried no water but fed with water from an external main, these vehicles had a formidable oil fire-fighting capability. Their stainless steel tank (foam compound severely corrodes mild steel) had two compartments to carry 1,800 gallons of fluoroprotein foam and 595 gallons of aqueous film-forming foam. They were fitted with an Albany engine-driven pump to self-load and to feed the proportioner. The bodywork was minimalist and was little more than a man stand and a monitor mounted at the rear.

While the Ford Transit, Bedford CF and Land Rover were still largely looking after the smaller chassis needs within the UK, mention should be made of what become the alternative to the Dodge Power Wagon as the basis for an appliance - the GMC K series. Again of American manufacture, they had the advantage of a longer chassis length and therefore the ability to carry the ever-increasing quantities of kit that the fire service of the day required. Three UK brigades took to this chassis as converted by HCB-Angus while other brigades had similar vehicles with conversions by other builders None of the HCB-Angus vehicles were pumping appliances but were built as rescue tender-type vehicles and, despite being rather on the long side, their road performance lent them to this type of work. Bedfordshire Fire Service had two, s6367, registered E933 YBH, and s6378, registered Y934 YBH. Hereford and Worcestershire Fire Brigade had three: s6369, registered 124 FCJ; s6379, registered E125 FCJ; and s6437, registered G781 FWP. Finally, Humberside Fire Service took just the one, s6395, registered F151 BAT. Shell (Malaysia) had one running as a foam tender, s6383, and the British Virgin

A number of emergency tenders were constructed for the Yorkshire brigades on the short wheelbase Dennis DS 153 chassis. This one was one of a pair (s6380.1–2) registered E788 and E799 LAJ for the North Yorkshire Fire Brigade. (*HCB-Angus Archive*)

A rear view of one of the group. This time it is s6403 again for the North Yorkshire Fire Brigade. Curves did not feature greatly on these appliances! (*HCB-Angus Archive*)

A steady stream of refinery vehicles was constructed over the years, each unique in its own way as the requirements of each refinery was met. This one was built for the Lindsey Refinery establishment on a Ford Cargo, s6410, registered F222 WPR. It carried two fire fighting compounds: 1,800 gallons of floroprotien foam compound and 600 of aqueous film-forming foam. (*HCB-Angus Archive*)

Islands also had a pair, one carrying 200 gallons of water in a pillow tank, s6441, and the other as a towing vehicle, s6442, making a total of nine chassis taken on.

The name Land Rover has appeared here several times, being a stalwart of small appliance construction and given all manner of treatments by the company. It has not usually gained much comment here in this narrative, as it is difficult to pick one from so many. However, one derivative is worthy of particular mention and this is the 6x4 and 6x6 conversions that the company bodied. The chassis extensions and axle additions were done by County Conversions on behalf of HCB-Angus and the chassis were then returned to Totton for building. The first of these was a strange vehicle for Leicestershire in 1982. Based on a 6x4 chassis and powered by the Rover V8 petrol engine, it was conceived as a forward control unit on the assumption that it would be first to the fire. It had a fire-fighting capability, with a front-mounted Godiva ACP pump fed from a 100-gallon water tank, short ladders and basic kit. It was, however, the addition at the rear of a small command and control space that was very unusual and made this a special appliance. The application was not a great success and the appliance was progressively downgraded, ending up as a towing vehicle for the brigade's inflatable boat. Registered BUT 906Y, the vehicle was built on s6201.

At the other end of the decade in 1989, the Rover Company had a pair of 6x4 appliances, s6438, registered G600 WAC, and s6458, registered H477 BKV. These were identical appliances running as full pumping vehicles with PTO-driven Godiva pumps, carrying 130 gallons of water, 25 gallons of foam compound and extension

As the Dodge Power Wagons came to be too small, a bigger vehicle was looked for. The answer was the GMC K30 series. Bedfordshire Fire and Rescue Service had a pair kitted as fast rescue tenders: s6367, registered E933 YBH, and s6378, registered E934 YBH. (*HCB-Angus Archive*)

Humberside Fire Brigade also had one, this time a CV30 version, registered F151 BAT, on s6395. Unlike the Dodges these had diesel engines, so they were a little less thirsty! (*HCB-Angus Archive*)

ladders as well as the usual small gear. Dorset Fire and Rescue Service took delivery of s6370, registered E367 PFX, based on a 6x6 version of the County Conversions chassis specifically for use off-road on the large areas of heath land in the county. While visually very similar to the Rover Company vehicles, it differed in not having a main pump but using a PTO-driven pump by Albany just feeding one hose reel, as large quantities of water are not required for fighting heath fires. Another two similar appliances of this 6x6 variation were ordered by Dorset: s6387.1 to 2, registered F338 and F339 VFX.

The last of this group (though within the next decade) were a pair of 6x6 Land Rovers for Zeutina Oil in Libya, s6513 and s6532. With a more straightforward box-type body as no ladders were carried, they were equipped with a main pump, the same as the Rover Company vehicles.

As described earlier, the demise of Bedford as a truck-making concern came as a bit of a shock to the whole coachbuilding industry, not just fire appliance builders. HCB-Angus had embraced the TL version of the faithful old truck, had modified its designs and supplied many appliances based on it, but had also been looking forward to a new chassis supplier. So when the end came for Bedford, the company was able to switch, while not exactly at a stroke, to a new baseline chassis provided by Volvo UK Ltd. This was the FL6.14 chassis, modified at the manufacturer as a fire chassis, i.e. with the ancillaries that normally hung on the outside of the chassis rails moved to a position which allowed the locker construction to take place. HCB-Angus designed yet another version of their sandwich PTO, the DC3, to use in the Volvo, fitting it between the engine and Allison auto gearbox.

Built to the basic JCDD specification for a water tender, the Volvo FL series was a light, responsive and compact vehicle that suited the needs of the brigades of the day. It offered a more positive and advanced technical specification than the Bedford it largely replaced.

The first brigade to operate some of this new breed was Dorset Fire and Rescue Service, who took on the demonstrator and three others, s6366.1–4, registered W999 MJT, E568 and E569 NRU and E336 OJT. Built without a combined tilt cab, the Volvo was only offered with a manufacturer's tilt cab and fixed crew cab. The new chassis was quickly adopted and many UK brigades ordered it for use in their fleets.

During the entire production period of frontline appliances HCB-Angus, in line with all other fire appliance manufacturers, had used the main engine to drive the fire pump and this drive was always by way of open drive shafts. Now, this poses some problems. Hooke joints, used to take the drive around corners, must be arranged in pairs and the angles severely limited, and the whole assembly balanced, if severe vibrations are not to be felt and damage done to bearings and the like. Not only this, but the position of the drive line precludes the possibility of getting water tanks dropped well into the chassis rails, which would have the advantage of lowering the centre of gravity. Dorset Fire and Rescue Service mooted the possibility of using a hydrostatic drive as a solution to both these problems. A hydraulic drive system consists of three parts: the generator (hydraulic pump), driven by the engine; valves, filters, piping, etc. (to guide and control the system); and the motor (hydraulic motor) to drive the machinery. Theoretically this

Land Rover appliances have not featured greatly on these pages but these next require a special mention, being six-wheelers. Leicestershire Fire Brigade ordered this rather strange machine, registered BUT 906Y (s6201). Specified as a light fire pump, it carries water and has a front bumper-mounted Godiva ACP pump, but also acted as a forward control unit – hence the cabin at the rear. The concept was not a success and the vehicle ended up as the brigade's boat trailer towing vehicle. (*HCB-Angus Archive*)

Dorset Fire and Rescue Service ordered two of these appliances on s6370.1–2, registered E367 and E368 PFX, specifically for their agility in tackling the heath fires the county suffers from so much. As they have a 6x6 drive configuration, the one-tonne Land Rover Defender is well up to the task. (*HCB-Angus Archive*)

Left: The business end of the Dorset Fire Service Land Rovers. The vehicle carried 130 gallons of water and has an engine-driven, high-pressure Albany pump feeding a fog gun. It also carries a Godiva light pump in a demount cradle at the rear. (*HCB-Angus Archive*)

Below: The sudden decision of Bedford to cease truck production left HCB-Angus short of a suitable chassis. Volvo was only too happy to step into the breach and HCB-Angus soon had a FL614-based appliance ready. The first order for Volvos came from the company's near neighbour Dorset, which placed an order for four on s6366.1–4. E999 MJT was one of the four seen here on station. (*Photographer unknown*)

F 354 RBJ was one of many further Volvo FL614 water tender and water tender ladders to come out of Totton. Suffolk Fire and Rescue Service ordered nine engines on s6424.1–4 and s6425.1–5, the two orders being registered sequentially as F351 – F359 RBJ. (*HCB-Angus Archive*)

An odd order was for a Volvo FL614 machine for Castellon in Spain. The chassis cab was obtained in Spain and brought to the UK for fitting out – hence the visor and deflectors. Built on s6446, it was an order that was not repeated. (*HCB-Angus Archive*)

The Dodge S66 chassis was used with some success in the industrial brigade market. F818 XJT, s6420, was built for Glaxo Pharmaceuticals Ltd, carrying 150 gallons of water and having a road engine-driven pump. (*HCB-Angus Archive*)

was sound; hydraulic pumps and drives were becoming more widespread (concrete mixer lorries and the like had been using them for some time) and the design is theoretically simple: a hydraulic pump driven direct from the power take-off, coupled to an identical item running as a motor attached directly to the fire pump, and the pair connected with flexible pipework full of oil running at high pressure, in this case 13 bar. In practice, things were not so simple. The mechanical parts had to rotate quickly (fire pumps run at several thousand revolutions per minute) and this meant a lot of oil movement, which in turn meant a lot of heat build-up. HCB-Angus took on the task of developing the system in conjunction with Volvo Hydraulics Ltd and after some technical difficulty, devised a system that worked but, among other things, required some locker space to be sacrificed for an oil reservoir. This was not good, as locker space was always at a premium.

Dorset Fire and Rescue Service took four of these vehicles initially, s6415.1–4, registered F153 to F155 XFX, and followed this order with a total of twelve more during the next few years. Interestingly, no other brigade took up this option on its appliances and HCB-Angus made no attempt to redesign the water tank so as to drop it further in the frame.

As the decade came to its end, other chassis were brought on board. The Dodge S66 was used a few times for lightweight appliances, s6420, registered F818 XJT, for Glaxo Pharmaceuticals for instance, and Mercedes became the appliance of choice for some UK brigades although the company had been using them for export appliances for

Mercedes was a chassis not to be ignored and this foam tender for Esso Fawley was built on s6423. The Mercedes 1936K carried 500 gallons of foam compound and 200 gallons of water delivered via hand lines and roof monitors. (*HCB-Angus Archive*)

On display is the business end of the Fawley appliance. No less than six hand lines can be used, together with a pair of roof monitors. (*HCB-Angus Archive*)

Occasionally customers required chassis that were not available in the UK. Tanzania Airport wanted this bonneted model of Mercedes so the local dealer had to import it especially for HCB-Angus to work on to create this rather good-looking crash tender. Built as s6162, no technical details are known. (*HCB-Angus Archive*)

some time, albeit in small numbers. For instance, bonneted Mercedes s6162, a chassis not available in this country, was imported, bodied and re exported to Julius Nyerere International Airport, the Republic of Tanzania's main airport, to see service.

Finally, for this era, one specific vehicle, which cannot be called an appliance because it was not for fire fighting, must be mentioned. Built in the early 1980s at the behest of the UK government of the day, s6434, registered NYL 713Y, was one of two ordered against a Home Office specification for what were euphemistically called 'crowd control units', otherwise water canon for dealing with riots. HCB-Angus and Carmichael were given a blank canvas on which to design a suitable vehicle against a general specification and they built one each. That built by HCB-Angus was on a Bedford TM 6x4 chassis and had the following details:

Body
Heavy sheet steel body skirted down to the ground with rubber sheeting
'No climb, no grip' construction
Reinforced glass with mesh protection
Crew cab, positive pressure with filtered air for the driver, commander and two operatives
The whole body fitted with wash down facilities from the main pump

Water system
2,000-gallon water tank with provision for dye to be added to the pumped water.
Godiva pump driven by an independent Ford engine
Two remotely controlled water cannon, turret mounted, with axial lights and TV cameras (recording in cab)
Normal fire equipment for water pick-up from mains or open water

The vehicles were built at the time of civil unrest caused by the recession of the time and the UK government's proposal to close coalmines. It is reported that the two vehicles were taken to the Metropolitan Police Training School at Hendon, where they were evaluated against several hundred 'rioting' policemen. Just what the outcome was is not reported but it was decided in 'high places' that the use of such vehicles in the UK was not politically sound and they were parked up, never to be used.

Above and overleaf: This aggressive-looking piece of work is just that! Produced for the UK government at the time of the industrial unrest of the 1980s, this crowd control unit (together with another produced by Carmichael) was seen as a possible solution. Underneath it is a Bedford TLM and it is comprehensively able to defend itself and its crew as well as attacking crowds with water – with or without dye. The water system was driven by an independent Ford unit, giving the operators and the driver autonomy of action. After a change of heart by the government the two vehicles were, after trials, parked up and left. (*HCB-Angus Archive*)

8
The 1990s - Final Years

The final years, despite everything, were busy. Production of Volvo-based water tenders continued apace but was seen as the root cause of the company's problems, situated as it was in an expensive part of the country, in terms of 'on-costs'. The basic production cost was more than could be expected as a sales price if the company was to remain competitive with the other major producers. However, much production was undertaken and some interesting vehicles produced, including some on Scania chassis for the first time, Leyland returning after many years and the Renault Midliner, also for the first time.

On the home front, the biggest individual order came from Kent Fire and Rescue Service with an order for nineteen water tender ladders on the Dennis SS239 chassis, being s6505.1–19, registered K819 to K838 SKE.

ICI, which had placed orders over the years with the company for a variety of special vehicles, continued to do so by ordering a pair of Volvo FL6.17-based appliances for the Wilton and Billingham works. Designated triple agent vehicles, they carried a fire-fighting medium for all eventualities, as you would expect for the diverse products these plants produced. These appliances carried 100 gallons of water, 500 gallons of foam compound, a 750 kg dry powder installation and a 500 kg BCF delivery system. A Godiva pump was installed for foam delivery via a monitor or four hand lines. Needless to say, they relied on the works mains for water during long periods of foam production. The two vehicles were s6450, registered H831 JPY, and s6480, registered J409 SEP.

The Mercedes MB122 water tenders, s6459.1–2, supplied to the Barbados Fire Service were an unfortunate pair of appliances. The crews for these appliances had been to the Totton works for a training period and the vehicles and crews returned to Barbados by sea, together with a representative of HCB-Angus, for a ceremonial handover. Unfortunately, an over-enthusiastic driver managed to crash his appliance into a wall during the handover demonstrations and the vehicle saw the end of the day with one front corner somewhat bent and the front suspension considerably damaged. The other of the pair saw its service career ended a few years later when it was overturned and written off.

The last Simon Snorkel to be bodied by the company was based on the Dennis F127 chassis and carried 85-foot booms. Destined for Bahrain, it carried body serial s6385.

The end of the line; the one of the last 'classic'-style Bedford TKG pair receives a final polish before delivery. Built for Suffolk Fire and Rescue Service on s6341.1–2 and registered D831 and D832 DPV, they were seen out of the factory with some nostalgia. (*HCB-Angus Archive*)

The arrival of the Bedford TL, with its headlamps in the bumpers configuration, necessitated a small revision to the HSC Bedford's front scuttle to accommodate this change. Here, one of the four ordered by Lincolnshire Fire and Rescue rests in the sun awaiting the attentions of the sign writer. Ordered as s6365.1–4, they were registered D801 – 803 XTL and E906 AVL. (*HCB-Angus Archive*)

Leyland chassis had featured in the early days of the company's history but had not featured for many, many years when the Zambian authorities placed two orders for water tender appliances. Two groups of eight appliances were constructed and shipped on s6462.1–8 and s6485.1–8. Kept simple, they featured the manufacturer's cab and a simple, box-construction crew/equipment body. Strangely, one of these vehicles was reported in use on the opposite side of the Atlantic some years later, serving with one of the West Indian brigades.

The Falkland Islands have particular problems, not least of which is the lack of a ready source of water for fire fighting, despite being surrounded by the Atlantic Ocean. Therefore, the Falkland Isles Fire and Rescue Service commissioned the construction of a large water carrier, s6399, based on an ex-MoD fuel tanker. The vehicle chosen was a 6x4 AEC TGRB that was already equipped with a twin-compartment, 4,800-gallon tank and locker provision between the cab and the tank. The locker was reworked and fitted with pumping equipment more suited to water than jet fuel and the tanks refurbished for rapid fill and the usual provision for overflow. The final product was suitably painted red and shipped out by sea.

Cornwall Fire Brigade had made the move to Mercedes chassis late in the 1980s with the purchase of four water tenders based on the M1272 chassis. These were s6448.1–4, registered G279 and G281 to G283 CRL, followed up in the last few years of the company by two pairs of Mercedes 1124AF-chassied appliances, s6526.1–2,

Kent Fire and Rescue Service's association with HCB-Angus goes back to the very beginnings of the company and late on in its life, the company was to secure a contact to build a large number of water tender ladders for the service. Built as two bodily identical batches on Dennis SS239 chassis, the first, s6505.1–17, were standard water tender ladders except that two were fitted with Rosenbaur pumps rather than Godiva and the second batch, on s6506.1–3, were fitted with the Godiva 1,000 gpm pump rather than the 500 gpm unit and the appliances were equipped with a roof monitor. The two batches were sequentially registered as K819 – K838 SKE. (*HCB-Angus Archive*)

A group of the Kent Dennis SS239 engines await delivery outside the works. (*HCB-Angus Archive*)

ICI Wilton ordered a triple agent vehicle on s6450, based on the Volvo FL617 chassis, registered H831 JPY (*top*). A typical chemical industries appliance, it carried water, foam and a dry powder installation. They were so pleased with the end product that, a few months later, they ordered an identical vehicle on s6490, registered J405 SEF (*above*).

registered L213 and L214 VRL, and s6527.1–2, registered L211 and L212 VRL. These were all described as midi water tenders because they were constructed as compactly as possible, better to negotiate the territory in which they operated. The only design concession was the reduction of water carrying capacity to 300 gallons from the more usual 400 gallons for water tenders. The last four were of 4x4 configuration, giving them a greater cross-country ability.

Mid Glamorgan Fire Service also took five of these tough 4x4 Mercedes, being s6492.1–5, registered J250 to J254 WBO, to go alongside their Scania appliances.

The MoD's last involvement with HCB-Angus was by way of a flurry of small orders for Volvo FL6.14-based water tender ladders. They were all identical but ordered over a period of time. There were eleven in all:

s6486: registered 44 KK 10
s6487.1–5: registered 44 KK 11–15
s6503.1 to 2: registered 76 KK 58–59
s6520.1 to 3: registered 82 KK 71–73

The north-west of England saw a couple of new types of chassis for some of their appliances. Greater Manchester Fire and Rescue Service chose the Renault M230 Midliner for an order for seven water tender ladders, s6510.1–7, registered K783 to

The Falkland Islands were in need of a substantial water carrier for their fire service, despite being surrounded by the Atlantic Ocean. This impressive-looking appliance was created from an ex-MoD fuel bowser. The fuel pumping system in the locker was replaced with water pumping equipment – a comparatively easy exercise. AEC TGRB was the chassis, with two compartments to the tank of 3,000 and 1,300 gallons respectively, the vehicle being built on s6499. (*HCB-Angus Archive*)

K789 ANC. The company saw this as a potential chassis for much future production as it was somewhat tougher than the Volvo FLs but not as large as the Scanias that were being offered by its competitors. The company spent a lot of time and effort getting these vehicles onto a sound manufacturing basis. As had been hoped, they turned out as solid, dependable appliances but further orders were not forthcoming. Cumbria Fire Service were looking for a compact, yet still full-specification water tender ladder and chose the Leyland DAF FA 45 chassis as a base, small enough to negotiate Cumbria's roads yet heavy enough to carry a full quota of water and kit. These were built on s6514.1–5, registered K477 FRM and L214 to L218 KAO. They appeared as attractive appliances, their small wheels and neat cabs belying their full specification. Jumping on the bandwagon, as it were, Vickers Shipbuilding and Engineering, Ltd in Barrow decided to have one of the same for its works brigade and no doubt got a good price due to the economies of scale. This one was built on s6515, registered K370 GRM.

As mentioned above, the Scania chassis was not favoured by HCB-Angus and only a handful passed through the company's hands during these last few years. All for the Glamorgan Brigades, the total production was made up by:

s6475: Scania P93H for West Glamorgan Fire Sevice, registered H562 OGK
s6491.1–2: Scania G93M for Mid Glamorgan Fire Service, registered J98 SNY and J652 STX
s6518.1–2 Scania G93M for West Glamorgan Fire Service, registered K516 and K517 BTX

One unusual supply by the company was of a Volvo FL6.14 appliance, s6493, to the requirements of the Castellon brigade in Spain. While otherwise a standard HCB-Angus product, it had ladders by Escaleros Servitja, a double extension of 6 metres and a pair of hook ladders, the latter of which had not carried by UK brigades for many years.

And so we come to the final year of production. During 1993, some thirty or more vehicles were ordered before the notice of closure came on 30 November, some for the UK market and some for foreign parts. Hampshire Fire and Rescue Service, with whom the company had enjoyed a special relationship over all the years of production, placed their final order for four water tender ladder Volvo FL 6.14s, s6531.1–4, registered L84, L85, L87 and L89 RTP. The last Bedfords, from Marshall of Cambridge, went off to the Nigerian National Petroleum Company in the form of a pair of Bedford M foam carriers, s 6533.1–2.

The last of the new orders for the UK were indeed special. Tyne and Wear Fire and Rescue Service ordered an emergency tender appliance, s6534, registered L202 ANL, which went on the run in 1994 and at the time of writing (summer 2011) is still on front line service.

The very last Totton-built appliance, s6537, registered L343 CEL, was one of the 4x4 Mercedes midi water tenders built for Dorset. After all its years of work with the service, the appliance was donated to a group of volunteers and has been driven all the way round the world, leaving the UK on 18 July 2010 and arriving back in London

Greater Manchester Fire and Rescue Service placed an order with HCB-Angus for seven water tender ladders registered K783 – K789 on s 6510.1–7 on the Renault M320 chassis, the Midliner. HCB-Angus was keen to develop this chassis for fire engine use, but the company never got to produce any further examples. (*Photographer unknown*)

The Scania P93H is generally regarded as a tougher truck and as such was favoured by some brigades, although few passed through HCB-Angus hands. This one, s6475, registered H562 MDW, was built for the West Glamorgan Fire Service. (*HCB-Angus Archive*)

Another Scania for a Glamorgan Fire Service, this time Mid Glamorgan, is one of a pair, s6491.1-2, registered J98 SNY and J625 STX. (*HCB-Angus Archive*)

Tyne and Wear Fire and Rescue Service ordered an emergency tender from the company to be based on the Volvo FL6 and it was delivered shortly before the company closed. Built on s6534, it was registered L202 ANL and at the time of writing, July 2011, is still on frontline service in Newcastle upon Tyne. (*Photograph Simon Rowley*)

The very last fire engine to leave HCB-Angus works. Mercedes 1124 s6537, registered L343 CEL, was ordered by Dorset Fire and Rescue Service to complete their acquisition of four of these similar 4x4 midi water tenders. This appliance, *Martha* as she is now known, now features in the *Guinness Book of World Records*, having completed a round-the-world trip of some 26,000 miles in support of a cancer charity. (*Photographer unknown*)

on 12 April 2011, a total of 267 days. 'Follow That Fire Engine' is dedicated to the memory of Garth Moore, who passed away on 18 July 2009 at the age of 63, after a battle with lung cancer. Garth was a fire fighter at Wimborne Fire Station in Dorset and dedicated his life to fighting fires and saving the lives of others over the course of his 33 years in the service. Martha, as the Mercedes came to be known, now features in the *Guiness Book of World Records* as the only fire appliance to have been driven around the world.

So production trickled to a halt and the works was auctioned off. Over 6,000 fire appliances and an unknown number of commercials were produced over a period of some seventy years. Exported around the world to over 100 countries, the name of HCB-Angus is known worldwide and respected by fire-fighters everywhere.

Postscript

There were three more orders, significantly all for foreign parts: a water tender for Tanzania, a triple agent vehicle on a Leyland Comet and a Land Rover appliance for one of the company's biggest customers, Nigeria. None of these vehicles entered production at Totton but were given to Saxon to build and wore that company's badge into service.

The Database

For logistical reasons it is not possible to include the Database of Fire Appliance Production 1948–1993 within this book, as it is some 6,500 lines long and in printed form is not easy to interrogate. If the reader would like to obtain a copy on a CD-ROM containing the full database then he should contact the author on this email address for further information:

aidanfisher@yahoo.com

Enquires will be dealt with promptly.